P9-DGW-617

SECURING DEMOCRACY

SECURING
DEMOCRACY

Why We Have an Electoral College

Edited by
Gary L. Gregg II

With an Introduction by
Senator Mitch McConnell

ISI BOOKS
Wilmington, Delaware
2001

Library of Congress Cataloging-in-Publication Data

      Securing democracy : why we have an electoral college /
edited by Gary L. Gregg —1st ed. —Wilmington, DE :
ISI Books, 2001.

     p. cm.

    ISBN 1-882926-65-x
     1. Electoral college—United States. 2. Elections—United States.
3. United States—Politics and government. I. Gregg, Gary L. II.
Why we have an electoral college

JK1976 .S43 2001   2001-89323
324.63 / 0973—dc21   CIP

Published in the United States by:

    ISI Books
    Post Office Box 4431
    Wilmington, DE 19807-0431
    www.isibooks.org

Manufactured in the United States of America

To Krysten

Contents

Preface

*S*ecuring Democracy has its ultimate origins in the time when I was in graduate school in the early 1990s. I noticed then that the general bias against the Electoral College was driven by ideology more than scholarship, and that this political ideology even seemed to bleed over into some of the scholarly literature on presidential elections. I did some basic spadework preparing the way for what I thought would soon be a definitive scholarly look at the origins of the Electoral College, a work I hoped would correct the misperceptions and misinformation in the literature. Other projects and several books crept in to vie for my time in the intervening decade between then and the 2000 presidential election.

When the results of that election became obscured in a blizzard of Florida chads and lawsuits, I regretted that my pen had not been swifter and that I had not written the book I had planned. In the hours and days following the closure of the polls last November, calls for the abolition of the Electoral College began. First it was the newly elected Senator Hillary Clinton. Then Republican Senator Arlen

Specter. Several members of the House of Representatives joined in with their own calls for reform and abolition. Columnists joined the chorus. Academics dug out their old manuscripts warning against "the coming debacle" and the danger of having a president who did not win the popular vote. At least one poll of the American people found fairly wide support for the abolition of the College.

But, as has been the case throughout American history, thoughtful voices were also raised in the College's defense. A few pundits and academics, taking a longer view of American political development, began pointing to the salutary effects the Electoral College has had for our political system. Theirs is the harder job, however. Those who argue for a direct national election can simply cry "democracy" and "majority rule" to make their point. Their slogans can fit on the back of a Volvo and are easily understood by the most casual observer.

The case for the Electoral College, on the other hand, is subtler and deeper. It requires an understanding of more than one election and a prudent concern for the long-term consequences of constitutional innovations. It requires more than a few op-eds and deserves more than a passing glance.

In the weeks following the 2000 election, it became evident that a more sustained analysis of the Electoral College and its place in American democracy was needed. With the strong support and encouragement of the editorial staff at ISI Books, I set out to bring together some of the more intelligent voices being raised in defense of the Electoral College for just such a sustained examination. I am grateful that those authors whose work is included in this book responded positively to my request and our publisher's demand to work at the academic equivalent of Mach speed.

The authors were quick but diligent. We all labored under a sense of profound gratitude to the men and women who over the years have been courageous enough to defend constitutional principles and processes in the face of consistent opposition and prevailing cultural trends. The result is the book you now have before you; we hope it will play some small part in future discussions of our electoral and constitutional system of presidential elections.

A number of people deserve a degree of credit for their help and support during the creation of *Securing Democracy*. Sherry Allen, Wanda Adams-Taylor, and Christopher McCloskey aided the creation of the manuscript for this book in a number of ways. Jeff Nelson and Jeremy Beer at ISI Books believed in the project from the beginning and never wavered in their support and in their labors. My students in the McConnell Scholars program at the University of Louisville were patient with me in the months I was preoccupied with the manuscript. Speaking of patience, Krysten, my wife of ten years, reminded me regularly of the importance of this book as we watched the post-election news from Florida and then supported me during the months it took to complete the project. I am particularly grateful for her love and support.

Of course, we all share an intellectual debt that runs back to the American Founding Fathers and beyond. We hope this volume is worthy of that debt and that it serves in some small way to remind our fellow citizens of the precious constitutional inheritance that is free government in America.

GARY L. GREGG II
LaGrange, Kentucky

Introduction

Mitch McConnell

During the debate over the ratification of the Constitution,
Alexander Hamilton began *Federalist* 68 by remarking that the
constitutional system for electing the president "is almost the only
part of the system, of any consequence, which has escaped without
severe censure or which has received the slightest mark of approbation from its opponents." How things would change! Since the
earliest days of the Republic, opponents have raised their scorn
against the Electoral College. President Andrew Jackson famously
called for its abolition as early as the 1820s, and its opponents have
only grown more strident as we have drifted in time and memory from
the Founding generation.

Weeks before the American people went to the polls last November, voices were raised against the Electoral College on op-ed pages
all over the nation. When the election bogged down near the swamps
of Florida during the early morning hours of November 8, one could
almost hear the challenges becoming more shrill and sustained.

Within a few days after the election, several prominent political leaders joined the call to sweep away our method of electing presidents.

The bonds of our union were tested in the aftermath of the Florida voting. Many Republicans found the process of deciphering dimpled and pregnant chads to be a violation of the rule of law. Democrats fought for continued recounts. African-American leaders charged that myriad election-day frauds had been perpetrated against black voters. The court battles in Florida and Washington that eventually brought an end to the weeks of suspense left no one truly satisfied. The process tested us, but it did not break our union, and soon our political life returned to normal with a new president and the peaceful transference of power. America is truly a resilient nation.

Whatever may have gone wrong in the Florida voting and its aftermath, we know two things for certain. First, the American people know more about the Electoral College than they did before. History and government classes discussed its intricacies with a renewed sense of its importance. Citizens who had never before thought about our constitutional processes now found themselves confronted with a system that must have seemed almost alien to most of them. This was a positive result; it is always good to encourage the American people to learn more about the constitutional order upon which our current freedom and prosperity have been built.

Immediately following the election, at least one poll showed that more than sixty percent of the American people supported a constitutional amendment to replace the Electoral College with a direct national election for president. These Americans were apparently in agreement with those politicians, intellectuals, and journalists who argued that the election had provided fresh evidence of major problems with our electoral process.

But far from being evidence of problems inherent in the Electoral College, the College is the only thing that kept us from an even worse national nightmare. Yes, the recount process and court battles in Florida were excruciating to watch and dragged on far too long. But can you imagine the situation without the Electoral College? What if we would have instituted, as so many have urged upon us, a direct national election? The difference between Al Gore and George W. Bush in the national popular vote was about 500,000 (less than that, even, in the first few days after the election). That is a difference of less than .5% of the votes cast. A few thousand votes here and a few thousand votes there could have changed that election result. The Electoral College served to center the post-election battles in Florida. Without it, I fully expect we would have seen vote recounts and court battles in nearly every state of the Union. Can you imagine the problems in Florida multiplied 10, 25, or even 50 times? Rather than being an argument against the Electoral College, the 2000 election was a strong and forceful warning against its abolition.

About the time I graduated from law school in 1967, a distinguished commission of the American Bar Association recommended that the Electoral College be abolished. Like the critics of the current hour, they wanted to replace it with a direct national election for president. What if—as is almost assured to occur in such a system, because of its encouragement of third parties—no candidate succeeded in earning a majority of the votes cast? If no candidate received at least 40 percent of the vote, said the commission, there would be a second election, a run-off election, among the top candidates. Just imagine going through two presidential elections every four years instead of just one!

The commission's proposal passed the House of Representatives in 1969, nearly passed the Senate in 1970, and was later endorsed by President Jimmy Carter. At the time I was fresh out of law school and working as a young legislative assistant to Senator Marlow Cook, who had me doing staff work in favor of abolishing the Electoral College. But the more I read and the more debates I listened to, the more convinced I became that Sam Ervin, the Democratic senator from North Carolina who was a principle defender of the Electoral College, was right and we were wrong. We can all be thankful that cooler heads prevailed at that hour.

However, that same ABA proposal continues to raise its head from time to time in Washington and on the op-ed pages. The ABA commission attacked our presidential election system as "archaic, undemocratic, complex, ambiguous, indirect, and dangerous." We heard the same charges again following the 2000 election. (As a lawyer, I have always found it ironic that a national group of legal professionals would dismiss anything for being old, complex, and not easily understood.) The essays that are contained in this book do a good job of dealing with these charges, and they also point us to those many positive aspects of the Electoral College that have heretofore either been ignored or gone unrecognized by its opponents. But before discussing the arguments found in the rest of this book, it is good to remind ourselves of exactly how the Electoral College system actually works in today's politics.

THE ELECTORAL COLLEGE TODAY

Electors are distributed to the states in the exact proportion that those states are represented in Congress. Each state gets the equivalent of its membership in the House of Representatives, which is based on population, plus its two senators, which are distributed to the states as autonomous and equal political entities. My state of Kentucky now has eight votes in the Electoral College—six representing our six seats in the House and two additional votes representing our membership in the Senate.

This method of vote distribution is the origin of the Electoral College bias that strengthens the influence of the smaller and more rural states; that is, every state is to some extent treated as an equal and autonomous political community because a portion of every state's votes represent its Senate representation, which is the same for California and Connecticut, Texas and Delaware. This is also the reason that one candidate can win the popular vote and another win the Electoral College vote, which of course is what happened in 2000. Al Gore won large majorities in urban areas of the Northeast and California, while George W. Bush won the votes of the South, Midwest, and Mountain West.

Al Gore, my old colleague in the Senate, finished with about 500,000 more votes than did George W. Bush. As we watched the results coming in on election night, however, it was clear that Bush was winning the popular vote all night as the polls closed from time zone to time zone—until we hit the West Coast. Gore picked up more than a million more votes in California than did Bush, and those votes are what put him ahead of Bush in the popular vote nationally. The electoral bias in favor of the smaller and more rural states, however, gave George W. Bush the presidency. One analysis even showed that Bush won areas with a landmass of more than 2.4 million square miles, while Gore garnered winning margins in areas with a landmass of just over 580,000. The men who created the Electoral College would have well understood this situation.

This is how we run our presidential elections. They are state-by-state battles to accumulate a majority in the Electoral College. To say that one candidate won the popular vote and another won the vote of the Electoral College misses the point. Neither in 2000 nor at any other time in American history has the goal of a presidential race been to win the national popular vote. If that were the goal, the electoral strategies of both candidates would have been very different. In efforts to maximize their raw vote totals, you would have seen George W. Bush spending much of his time in his own state of Texas, while Al Gore would have camped out in California. Their campaigns would have been different and the results would have been different. But that is not our system, and unless the Constitution is amended, it is not fair to overlay it with expectations and evaluations alien to that system.

When our citizens go to vote, they are technically not voting directly for president. Rather, they are voting for a slate of electors who are pledged to vote for a particular presidential candidate. In Kentucky last year, more of my fellow citizens and I voted for George W. Bush for president than voted for Al Gore, and so the eight electors who had pledged their support for Bush were chosen to cast their votes for us in the Electoral College. As in every state except Maine and Nebraska, Kentucky gives its votes in a "winner-take-all" system. Bush won the majority of the popular votes and so won all the Electoral College votes from the state. This was what was at stake in the Florida recounts (or "revotes," as some of us saw it). The winner of the popular vote in Florida, even if by only a few hundred votes out of the millions cast, would win all 25 of the state's electoral votes and therefore the presidency.

These electors, who tend to be party activists and loyal supporters of the presidential candidate in their state, meet in their state capitals several weeks after the election. There they cast two ballots— one for president and one for vice president. Those ballots are then sealed and sent to Congress to be opened and counted in January. Are these electors free to vote for whomever they wish? The simple answer is, yes. Though many states technically require them to vote as they have pledged, some do not have penalties attached to that mandate, and it is not quite clear that these requirements, if tested, could meet constitutional muster. After all, the Founders intended to leave these electors free to use their own best judgment, so could they now be legally bound without a constitutional amendment? There have been a few of what we have come to call "faithless electors" in American history, but none of them have ever really even come close to changing the outcome of an election. Last year, one delegate from Washington, D.C., did not vote for Al Gore, to whom she was pledged, as a protest against the District of Columbia not having full representation in Congress. But it's not clear that if this elector's vote had been the deciding vote she would have been so eager to break her pledge.

All the votes are then counted in a joint session of Congress. The incumbent vice president of the United States, who also serves as the president of the Senate, presides over the counting of the electors' votes. I was privileged to take part in this process after the most recent election, when Vice President Gore had the duty of counting the votes that made his rival president. What a difficult constitutional burden this must have been! Despite repeated disruptions from some of his own supporters, who he had to rule out of order time and time again, the Vice President seemed to handle this difficult situation with the good humor and dignity befitting our constitutional regime.

One candidate must receive a majority of the electoral votes cast to become president. In America today, that magical number is 270 (out of the 538 total electoral votes). George W. Bush got just 271 in 2000. But what if he had not? What if, in a close national election such as this one, there had been a viable third party candidate who could have garnered some electoral votes, keeping either of the other two candidates from getting a majority?

The constitutional back-up plan would have the House of Representatives choose the president and the Senate choose the vice president. The House would have to choose among the top three vote-getters in the Electoral College and would vote as state delegations, not as individuals. Each state would have but one vote for president and a majority of those state votes would be required for a president to be elected. The Senate would then choose the vice president from the top two contenders for that office. This has happened before, but not in well over a century. In fact, the last time the choice of president went to the full House, my predecessor as a senator from Kentucky, the great statesman Henry Clay, played a leading role in the choice of John Quincy Adams over Andrew Jackson.

Is the Electoral College method of presidential selection the easiest to understand or the most efficient in its execution? No. But our system is not designed to be simple and efficient. It is designed to promote good government and legislation that forwards the common good of a large and diverse nation. For two centuries it has done a pretty good job at that. Every day when I walk into my Senate office, I am thankful for the complexities and inefficiencies that have contributed to the freedom and prosperity we know in America. Though it may never have functioned as intended, the Electoral College has been the linchpin of American political prosperity. It has formed our political parties, moderated our more extreme elements, and forged the presidential campaigns that have given direction to our ship of state.

OUTLINE OF THE BOOK

Securing Democracy is not an exhaustive attempt to chronicle every aspect of the importance of the Electoral College in American politics. Indeed, one could never really outline all the subtle ways constitutional processes like the Electoral College contribute to our life as a nation. Even the most accomplished social scientist or philosopher could not unravel the tangled web of culture and constitutionalism that forms our union. The nineteenth-century Frenchman Alexis de Tocqueville probably came as close as is humanly possible with his classic *Democracy in America*. But we do not undertake such a Herculean task here.

Nor does this book attempt an exhaustive accounting of every possible constitutional and statutory change that could be made in our system of presidential elections. (Some, for instance, would seem salutary. Personally, I would support efforts by the states that would bind their electors to vote the way they pledged. Other changes, such as states moving to systems of proportional distribution like the ones Maine and Nebraska have, would seem to mitigate the benefits of the

Electoral College as it exists today.) Rather, the essays collected here provide interesting and penetrating arguments for the importance of the Electoral College in American life. Collectively, these finely honed arguments should cause us all to pause and consider the long-term potentialities of a rush to judgment against our venerable presidential election system.

There may be some overlap in the arguments of the authors—a critical reader may even be able to find some disagreements among them—but it is clear that, when taken together, these scholars have an uncommonly deep and sophisticated understanding of the nature of American politics and its foundations in American constitutionalism. It is my hope that they will receive a wide readership among public figures, academics, and that engaged public that forms the backbone of our republic.

Gary Gregg begins the volume with an outline of the origins of the Electoral College at the Constitutional Convention and its defense in the *Federalist Papers*. To many, questions of origins are arcane and irrelevant. In his essay, however, Gregg demonstrates how an understanding of the origins of an institution can cast vital light on contemporary deliberations. Though he does not put it quite like this, I think his essay demonstrates that the Electoral College has served America well because it is built upon the nation's very foundation-stones. Though it may not function as the Founders intended, it has worked because it is based upon those principles upon which our Founders stood—federalism, the rule of law, and representative government.

George Washington was unanimously selected the first president of the United States in 1788 and 1792. The Electoral College functioned as intended in those two elections, because it settled upon the man most fit for the job. By 1800, however, the Electoral College began to break down. The American party system that George Washington fought so hard to discourage had been birthed in the disagreements between Thomas Jefferson and James Madison on the one hand and John Adams and Alexander Hamilton on the other. The Electoral College would never again function as intended.

In the second chapter, elections expert Andrew Busch outlines the development of the Electoral College from the great crisis following the election of 1800 through the democratization of the Electoral College in the states, and he explicates the controversial presidential elections of the nineteenth century, which in some ways set the stage for the events following the 2000 vote.

One of the more important aspects of the Electoral College is its recognition of the individual states as states. Though it has undeniably been the trend in modern America to look to the federal government for solutions to societal problems, the Electoral College reminds us both of the important role the Framers reserved to the states and the role the states continue to play in American politics. In his essay, James Stoner points out how important the Electoral College is to our continuing recognition of the states as guardians of something more fundamental than their roles as mere administrative units. He also reminds us how important the nexus between the Electoral College and the states has been in the democratization of American politics.

"America at its best matches a commitment to principle with a concern for civility." I was on the dais with the newly inaugurated President George W. Bush when he uttered those words as part of his eloquent inaugural address. On that cold and rainy Washington day, the new president captured a core element that has helped sustain the American political experiment for more than two hundred years: civility. Though it may not be immediately obvious, the Electoral College has contributed to the civility that has been a hallmark of most of our political history. It has contributed to the successful competition of our two broad political parties in almost every state and every region. It has dampened the candidacies of radical sectional candidates and demagogues. It has contributed to our politics being a little less fierce and a lot more productive than would otherwise be the case. It has, as Paul Rahe points out in Chapter IV, "moderated our political impulse."

In classical political thought, from the Greeks and Romans to the Founding era, political parties were held to be the scorn of free government. George Washington famously warned us to avoid such institutions in his Farewell Address, which is still read every year in the United States Senate. And yet, former President Washington had barely had time to rest beneath his shade trees at Mount Vernon before the American party system came to life. There are some—especially among our nation's youth—who continue to hold that our political parties are a blight on the body politic. But, unlike Washington, they argue that our parties are too moderate, that they are but two sides of the same loping and aimless mule.

Most of us, however, have come to realize that the two-party system seems to work very well and contributes to our political stability and happiness as a nation. In the fifth chapter, Michael Barone, that astute observer of contemporary politics, discusses the Electoral College as one of only two institutional supports of our two party system.

Without it as a stabilizing force, we might very well become a nation of fractured and radical parties unable to govern.

My former colleague in the Senate, Daniel Patrick Moynihan, rose to the Electoral College's defense in an address on the floor of the Senate more than two decades ago. The occasion was a debate on Senate Joint Resolution 28, one of the perennial attempts to eliminate the Electoral College and replace it with a direct popular election for president. A revised version of his sage warnings is included here as Chapter VI. In typical Moynihan fashion, he weaves historical details with philosophic nuance to cut to the core of the matter in such proposals, and he asks us to consider how close to the taproot of American democracy our innovators unknowingly hack.

In a similar vein, Michael Uhlmann warns in Chapter VII that because the Electoral College plays a critical role in our constitutional order, we endanger that order's coherence if we abolish the College. Appeals to honor the "will of the people," Uhlmann argues, can be as hazardous as they are misleading. Walter Berns, perhaps the one man who can claim the title of Dean of Electoral College Scholars, contributes the Afterword to this volume. He ends by asking us to consider the *outputs* of our elections as much as we do the *inputs*. Critics of the Electoral College, he points out, only seem concerned with electoral processes, voting mechanisms, and perceived violations of some magical elixir called "one-man, one-vote." Where, he asks us to consider, is the concern for the outputs of our system? Does it matter at all what kind of president our electoral process produces? Should we not be concerned that radical changes in the process may well lead to radical changes in the men who would inherit our greatest public trust?

Fittingly, *Securing Democracy* ends where it began, with the foundations of the Electoral College in the political theory of the Founders. Appendix I contains the constitutional elements of the Electoral College found in Article II and the Twelfth Amendment. James Madison's classic exposition of our compound republic in *Federalist* 39 and Alexander Hamilton's discussion of the Electoral College found in *Federalist* 68 are reprinted in the second appendix.

Anyone concerned with the future of our great nation would do well to consider the subtle and often overlooked contributions the Electoral College has made to American public life. These cannot be rendered into a six-second sound bite or be reduced to a bumper sticker slogan, but they are real and remain vital. Thanks to Gary Gregg and the contributors here collected, we now have a readily available reminder that the Electoral College has been responsible for much good and very little ill in American history. After more than two hundred years of political prosperity, how much more could we ask of any institution designed by human hands?

Chapter I

The Origins and Meaning of
the Electoral College

Gary L. Gregg II

Its critics and supporters both have it right. The Electoral College
does not work as it was intended to work by the Framers of our
Constitution. But if it does not function as intended, then how was
it intended to function?

This is a serious question with important implications for our
understanding of American democracy and presidential elections.
But despite its importance, scholars and pundits have given little attention to this basic concern. Most have either dismissed the question—as they dismiss the Electoral College itself—as archaic and uninteresting, or they have been satisfied to accept the prevailing notion
about its origins without evidence or serious scrutiny. Both tendencies are unfortunate and lead to a very thin appreciation for the system and its founding principles.

The origins of the Electoral College are more obscure than they
should be, not only because most scholars and political activists have
found the subject uninteresting, but also because many have accepted

an interpretation that says the Framers of the Constitution under-stood that the Electoral College would work to elect General Washington to be the first president but then would not likely work again. The College was, according to this understanding, a type of political mirage meant to conceal the true nature of presidential selection. That is, after Washington's election, the Electoral College would deadlock on a regular basis and throw the real selection of the president into the House of Representatives.[1]

Despite a considerable lack of evidence, this "designed to fail" interpretation of the origins of the Electoral College has crept through the scholarly literature, with author after author accepting it without question. It has also found its way into American government textbooks, in which the Electoral College is typically introduced to students not only as an institution that is not useful for our own time, but also as one that was never even intended to work at all. It's no wonder that our commentators and our citizenry have found it easy to dismiss our constitutional mechanism for selecting presidents.

THE CONSTITUTIONAL CONVENTION

The mode of selecting the chief executive was one of the more difficult problems that occupied the minds of the men assembled during the hot summer of 1787. The question was voted on and assumed to be closed a number of times during the Convention, only to rise again and again to stir up the proceedings. The question of how to elect the executive was central to the work of the Founders, since executive power itself presented a conundrum for the age of democracy and kingship.

The members of the Constitutional Convention strove to achieve a delicate tension in the mode to be used to choose the executive officer. They did not have the luxury of taking a simple course or hubristically adhering to one ideological principle at the exclusion of the lessons of history and other important values. As was the case with the entire constitutional order they designed, they had to create a balanced approach that was at once innovative in its application and prescriptive in its design.

Three basic (and in many ways competing) values animated the Convention with respect to the mode of selecting our chief executive. First, the system would need to be based upon the sound principles of the revolution. That is, it would need to find its legitimacy in the revolution's basic recognition that the people and their communities are ultimately the source of power. It would have to be republican. Second, the system would have to be so structured as to allow the president to be sufficiently independent from other entities; only then could he act his part with vigor and resolve. Third, the method of selection would need to be designed so as to encourage the choice of a person with the proper character for the high executive office. These three core values—republicanism, independence, and virtue—guided the design of the Electoral College. With this in mind, we can better understand its genius.

Various specific modes of electing the president were proposed during the Constitutional Convention, most attempting to achieve some balance between the three oft-competing goals. Though there were numerous specific manifestations of these programs, each can be placed into one of three general categories. Either they provided for popular election, election by the national legislature (or a part thereof), or election by some version of a specially chosen body of electors or other non-national figures (such as state governors). Given that our task is to come to grips with the origins of the Electoral College method of selection, it is useful to briefly explore the alternatives that developed.

THE CASE FOR POPULAR ELECTION

Polls have shown that a majority of Americans would support the replacement of the Electoral College with a direct popular election for president. In 1969 such a proposal even passed the House of Representatives, amply demonstrating that simple majoritarianism will always have an allure in a political system that values popular sovereignty and voting as highly as ours does. Simple, clear, easily understood, and comporting with our self-understanding as a democracy, majoritarianism has been the siren call of progressive historians for decades. But it has also appealed to many others throughout American history.

Was such an idea completely alien to the Founders? Were the men of Philadelphia elitists with an abiding fear of the people, as many historians have charged? The answer is complex, as is the political system they created. Yes, the Founders considered and debated the direct popular election of the president. And no, such a system did not gain much support at the Convention. But a careful look at the debates at the Convention and in subsequent ratifying conventions belies the notion that the Founders were simply undemocratic and distrustful of popular rule.

Direct popular election for president was the subject of two explicit votes by the Convention; on both occasions it was overwhelmingly defeated. On July 17, Gouverneur Morris made a motion to have the president elected by the people, but only Morris's own delegates from Pennsylvania voted in its favor. And again, on August 24, a popular election proposal was moved by Maryland's Daniel Carroll. It was defeated without any discussion at all, and with but two states supporting the idea.

The two most regular and articulate members to speak on behalf of popular election were Morris and his fellow Pennsylvanian James Wilson. Wilson first apprehensively raised the possibility on June 1, though he openly feared that "it might appear chimerical."[2] Indeed, no one even seems to have felt it necessary to immediately respond to his thoughts until he rose for a second time to declare his plan, in response to which George Mason, voicing support but finding such a mode impractical, suggested postponing the discussion until Wilson "might have time to digest it into his own form."[3] Ironically, what Wilson would propose the next day would in actuality be closer to the eventual Electoral College system than a direct popular vote: to have the people choose a representative from their district, who would then serve as one of the immediate electors for president.

A direct popular election of the president would of course adhere to the necessity that the system be republican. Such a system would also help encourage the president to be more independent and free to act than if he were elected directly by the national legislature, which was one of the most often proposed methods of selection. In fact, each time popular selection was raised as a possibility, it was in reaction to the Convention having entrusted the legislature with such an important power. But would a system of direct election by a national populace result in the selection of a president most fit for office, while also being representative of the genius of the political system itself?

Here again, the record is complex. Some delegates spoke in favor of direct popular election as likely to result in a good choice. Morris, for instance, said, "If the people should elect, they will never fail to prefer some man of distinguished character"; that is to say, they would choose someone of "continental reputation."[4] Others, such as Virginia's George Mason, were not so confident in the public.[5] What is more, many of the Founders' concerns about direct popular election involved electoral dynamics and political balances more than animus toward the public. A fear of demagoguery, a concern about competing favorite-son candidates in the states, logistical and procedural concerns about a single national election, and a need to adhere to the tensions and balances of the political system they were creating seem to have conspired against a direct election as much as any concern about the public's fitness to choose.

THE CASE FOR LEGISLATIVE SELECTION

As the vote counting, and recounting, crept forward in Florida after the election of November 7, 2000, fears began to be raised in Washington and across the country that 2000 might just be the year that the "nightmare scenario" would come true. The House of Representatives might be called to choose the president of the United States. The Supreme Court's decision to stop the recounts in select Florida counties saved Congress from having to make such a choice— and saved us all from having to witness the House of Representatives deal with this responsibility. But the Founders themselves had established the system whose back-up mechanism would be that legislative selection almost everyone hoped to avoid.

As I said earlier, some interpreters have claimed that the system of presidential election outlined in Article II of the Constitution was designed as a type of grand political shell game. On paper it would seem the president would be elected by a select group close to the people in the states, but in reality, the argument goes, it was established to routinely fail and send the actual selection of the president to the House and the selection of the vice president (perhaps) to the Senate. A close look at the Constitutional Convention and the writings of the Founders, however, provides little evidence for this interpretation.

It is true that the delegates at the Constitutional Convention did vote to have the president selected by the national legislature (or some part thereof) a number of times during the Convention. This would seem to be evidence for those who argue that the House was supposed to have routinely made the presidential choice. But if one attends closely to the context in which such votes were taken, one can expose this argument as false.

Connecticut's Roger Sherman would support legislative selection in the hopes of "making him [the president] absolutely dependent on that body"; he found independence in the executive to be "the very essence of tyranny."[6] But Sherman is worth quoting precisely because he is so unrepresentative of thought represented at the Constitutional Convention. The overwhelming number of the other delegates shared Montesquieu's belief that the concentration of power into *any* single entity constituted the essence of tyranny. They would agree with James Madison's statement that "If it be a fundamental principle of free Govt. that the Legislative, Executive & Judiciary powers should be *separately* exercised; it is equally so that they be *independently* exercised." And he went on, "There is the same & perhaps greater reason why the Executive shd. be independent of the Legislature, than why the Judiciary should: A coalition of the two former powers would be more immediately & certainly dangerous to public liberty."[7]

This basic commitment to a system of independent and separated powers pervaded the Convention and was one of the most fundamental goals when constructing the executive office. To a number of delegates this concern mitigated against any form of legislative selection. To others, it could be overcome through properly constructing the institution to build a degree of insulation between the president and the legislature.

Thus, the Convention sought to provide the president with certain institutional safeguards which, it was argued, would protect him from an overbearing legislature. Among the safeguards mentioned and subject to votes within the context of legislative selection were: giving the president a certain and fixed salary that the legislature could neither raise nor diminish; having a special committee of the legislature (perhaps even chosen by lot, as in James Wilson's proposal of July 24) choose the president and then disband; or having the legislature choose the president initially, but having incumbent presidents be elected by some other body so that they would not be beholden to the legislature for re-election.

The two most serious and regularly occurring proposals, however, were to subject the president to term limits and to make each term lengthy. These proposals often combined into a single six-year term for the president. However, to many, this medicine proved worse than the disease. Gouverneur Morris, for instance, argued that any kind of term limit on the president would encourage him to "make hay while the sun shines," while others spoke of the problems inherent in a lengthy term.[8]

Support for legislative selection was almost always expressed in combination with one or more of these institutional innovations. And when such safeguards were not present, support for a legislative mode of selection rapidly diminished. As James Wilson would put it starkly, "[It] seems to be the unanimous sense that the Executive should not be appointed by the Legislature, unless he be rendered in-eligible a 2d. time."[9] Following Wilson, James Madison went further:

> It is essential then that the appointment of the Executive should either be drawn from some source, or held by some tenure, that will give him a free agency with regard to the Legislature. This could not be if he was to be appointable from time to time by the Legislature. It was not clear that an appointment in the Ist instance [even] with an ineligibility afterwards would not establish an improper connection between the two departments.[10]

Thus, if one looks closely at the debates during the Constitutional Convention and the votes of the men who drafted the Constitution, one can see quite clearly that there is little evidence for the thesis that the Electoral College was a jerry-rigged system designed to regularly "fail" and send the ultimate decision to Congress. The Founders were too concerned to make the president independent of the legislature to agree to such a scheme of legislative selection, unless the president could be insulated from legislative control. Whenever the Convention demonstrated a commitment to legislative selection, it was always within the context of just such presidential insulation—usually in the form of term limits or a single, lengthy term. Except for the minor element of the legislature not being able to raise or cut a president's salary once he is in office, none of these institutional safeguards were included in the Constitution of 1787.

To assume that the Electoral College was just a throwaway institution the Framers realized would fail is to argue that the delegates completely abandoned all their concerns expressed throughout the summer concerning legislative tyranny. Such a reading goes against all the evidence.

A THIRD WAY: THE BIRTH OF THE ELECTORAL COLLEGE

With both direct popular election and election by the national legislature having proven to be problematic, a number of delegates argued for one or another version of a "third way" that would avoid the problems of the other two. In each of these proposals, specially chosen electors or other elected officials were to choose the president. And various modes were suggested for selecting the electors—from popular election, to selection by the state legislators or executives, to allowing the states to choose the mode of selecting the electors themselves (the latter solution would eventually be incorporated into Article II of the Constitution). Elbridge Gerry even suggested that the state legislators—and on a separate occasion that the state governors—be empowered to directly choose the chief magistrate.[11]

The electoral compromise position that eventually became part of the ratified Constitution was hammered out by Brearley's "Committee of Eleven," which reported to the Convention on September 4. Before the Committee reported its changes, the plan had been for the president to be chosen by legislative selection and to serve a single, seven-year term. As Roger Sherman noted almost immediately, the plan set forth by the committee would eliminate the ineligibility for re-election that was part of the plan of legislative selection, and it would also ensure the president's independence. After Madison voiced a concern about the voting methods of the contingency elections in Congress, Edmund Randolph and Charles Pinckney asked for a detailed explanation of the change in mode of election. Gouverneur Morris rose to express the Committee's views as well as his own, and Madison's notes of his remarks deserve a full recounting here:

> The Ist. was the danger of intrigue & faction if the appointmt. Should be made by the Legislature. 2 the inconveniency of an ineligibility required by that mode in order to lessen its evils. 3 The difficulty of establishing a Court of Impeachments, other than the Senate which would not be so proper for the trial nor the other branch for impeachment of the President, if appointed by the Legislature, 4. No body had appeared to be satisfied with an appointment by the Legislature. 5. Many were anxious even for an immediate choice by the people—6—the indispensable necessity of making the Executive independent of the Legislature.—As the Electors would vote at the same time throughout the U.S. and at so great a distance from each other, the great evil of cabal was avoided.[12]

What we see here in stark relief is Morris's summation of the motivations of the Committee, which hinges upon the undesirability of legislative selection. If they would have retained legislative selection they would have had to keep the re-election ineligibility requirement, which raised considerable problems of its own, such as the negation of the incentive for good behavior that some delegates mentioned would come with mandatory rotation or a limit on terms. Importantly, five of the six elements listed by Morris directly relate to the relationship between the executive and the legislature and the problems with allowing the latter to choose the former.

Morris's summation, which was not contradicted by any of the other members of the Committee, is significant evidence that the Founders did not intend the national legislature to routinely select the president. In sum, the Electoral College was not some ignoble compromise. It was not designed as some sort of constitutional tissue paper that for a time would cover the fault lines of the Convention only to dissolve away with the passing of Washington from the public stage. It was not, to wit, designed routinely to fail and send the selection of the president into the House of Representatives, as some of the College's critics continue to contend.

THE ELECTORAL COLLEGE AND THE FOUNDING PRINCIPLES OF AMERICAN GOVERNMENT

The Electoral College was to be a method of electing the president that in many ways would closely resemble the constitutional system writ small. The selection of a good man to be president, it was hoped, would work similarly to the way good public policy was supposed to emerge from the political system—that is, through the efforts of the most qualified people working under conditions that would encourage mature discussions. In the case of the political system, the desired end was public policy that would not threaten the system or any one part of it and would further the national good. Likewise, it was hoped that the Electoral College would result in a president with the qualifications and interests necessary to serve the public well. Properly understood, the Electoral College and its origins point to the ideas and values that undergird the entire American constitutional system as these were embedded in the foundations of the Electoral College itself.

Free Government:
Republicanism, Responsibility, and Responsiveness

The Founders were republicans. They were dedicated to a political system that would be based on "the consent of the governed" and that would be representative in form and function. The men that held the power to make decisions for society would be representatives of the people that were somehow accountable to them and would not be likely to threaten either their liberties or those of their freely chosen state and local governments. James Madison would define a "republic" as

> [a] government which derives all its powers directly or indirectly from the great body of the people, and is administered by persons holding their office during pleasure for limited periods, or during good behavior. It is *essential* to such a government that it be derived from the great body of society, not from an inconsiderable proportion or a favored class of it.... It is *sufficient* for such a government that the persons administering it be appointed, either directly or indirectly, by the people; and that they hold their appointments by either of the tenures just specified.... [emphasis in original][13]

Once we remember that the American Founders were not monarchists or antidemocratic, we can understand that there can be a diversity of electoral types that are legitimate in a representative system of government, and the less likely we may be to assume (as is the trend in our contemporary political culture) that direct democracy is the only legitimate electoral form.

Of the constitutional system designed to elect the president, Alexander Hamilton would write in *Federalist* 68, "It was desirable that the sense of the people should operate in the choice of the person to whom so important a trust was to be confided." The Founders believed it important that the people's best judgment should be felt in the presidential election system. But they were also very concerned with the product of the system. The inputs must be republican and must adhere to solid principles of free government. To the Founders, however, that did not require a one-size-fits-all mass democratic polity. The system the Founders settled upon was infused with "the sense of the people" while adding elements of other values and institutions that combined to produce presidents most likely to serve the common good.

And how would they serve the common good? At least in part, presidents would serve the nation in a manner similar to what then-Senator John F. Kennedy would immortalize 150 years later in his book *Profiles in Courage*.[14] They would serve the public good by resisting the temporary gales and gusts of public thought that are contrary to that public good. Rather than requiring elected officials to do what is popular, Alexander Hamilton would argue, "The republican principle demands that the deliberate sense of the community should govern the conduct of those to whom they intrust the management of their affairs; but it does not require an unqualified complaisance to every sudden breeze of passion or to every transient impulse which people may receive from the arts of men, who flatter their prejudices to betray their interests."

Hamilton would go on to lay the foundations of a type of leadership that seems to become more difficult every year, with the proliferation of public opinion polling and the dependence of presidential success on the shifting sands of the public mind:

When occasions present themselves in which the interests of the people are at variance with their inclinations, it is the duty of the persons whom they have appointed to be the guardians of those interests to withstand the temporary delusion in order to give them time and opportunity for more cool and sedate reflection. Instances might be cited in which a conduct of this kind has saved the people from very fatal consequences of their own mistakes, and has procured lasting monuments of their gratitude to men who had courage and magnanimity enough to serve them at the peril of their displeasure.[15]

Republican government demands our elected officials be *responsible* for their conduct but not that they be immediately and robotically *responsive* to every turn of the public mind. Because it is composed of a temporary body of top citizens, the Electoral College seems designed to encourage presidents who would serve in the way Hamilton indicates, while it also constantly reminds them that they will be held responsible for the results of their actions at least every four years (in addition to the ever-present threat of impeachment and removal).

The Electoral College also reminds us of an alternative to today's dominant political ethic, which equates the immediate election of the people—pure and simple majoritarianism—with good government. The Founders held to no such simple and dogmatic formula. They insisted that the new government they created be free and rest on the firm foundations of republicanism, but they were equally concerned that the government be good. In their assumption that the election process itself is more important than the president produced, the critics of the Electoral College (and to a large extent our political culture itself) seem to have adopted a reverse utilitarianism: "the means

justify the ends." But the Founders strove to balance their concerns
between process and product. To paraphrase Walter Berns's argument at the conclusion of this book, why has there never been a critic
of the Electoral College who has argued that a direct national election would produce *better* presidents?

And here I think the Founders are particularly instructive. Without challenge, we have come to assume that direct and unfiltered
democracy is always right in every case and in every situation. We
have come to see it as the only really legitimate way of conducting
free government, and we have even expanded that basic ethical
premise into the routinization of public opinion polls to gauge the
"legitimacy" of public figures and policy options. But the existence of
the Electoral College gives us the opportunity to pause and question
those assumptions, and in so doing to revisit the foundations of our
republic in a complex and representative form of government.

Virtue

Some have contended that the American Founders were largely
unconcerned about the quality of office holders in the American
political system. Rather, the argument goes, they sought to establish
a system in which the ambitious would check the ambitious and not
much would be accomplished. In such a way a stable political system
would be produced. This is a common misreading of the Founders'
project and of the political theory of their time.

Far from being unconcerned about the men who would take
positions of influence and prestige, the Founders were very concerned
about the qualities, character, and knowledge the nation's elected
presidents would possess; in short, they wanted to ensure that the

chief executive would possess that modicum of virtue necessary for free government to flourish. And this goal is not unique to the presidency. It is actually characteristic of in the dominant political theory of the time. Indeed, James Madison would write in *Federalist* 57 that "[t]he aim of every political constitution is, or ought to be, first to obtain for rulers men who possess most wisdom to discern, and most virtue to pursue, the common good of the society; and in the next place, to take the most effectual precautions for keeping them virtuous whilst they continue to hold their public trust."[16]

The Electoral College method of electing the president was in part designed to maximize the chance of having such a leader elected president. Alexander Hamilton maintained that the system would select "some fit person" to be president.[17] The means of selection, the Electoral College, would produce the desired end, the election of a recognized and experienced leader who would administer the executive branch as well as serve as a fitting symbol of national unity. Such a person would be found through a system that was deliberative, republican, and decentralized.

Though perhaps a bit overblown in his rhetoric, Alexander Hamilton seemed to believe that the Electoral College system was so well constructed as to afford "a moral certainty that the office of President will seldom fall to the lot of any man who is not in an eminent degree endowed with the requisite qualifications."[18] It is no accident, and is quite instructive to contemplate, that the only two times the Electoral College method was called into service and worked as intended it settled unanimously on George Washington.

Time and Deliberation

The Founders were convinced that good decisions are more likely to be made when people take time to think, discuss, and deliberate with one another. And so they established a system designed to encourage these processes to occur before public policy decisions were made. As Alexander Hamilton would write, "The oftener the measure is brought under examination, the greater the diversity in the situation of those who are to examine it, the less must be the danger of those errors which flow from want of due deliberation, or of those missteps which proceed from the contagion of some common passion or interest."[19]

Thus, the House of Representatives would be constituted of diverse men from various regions who would have to work together to produce legislation. Each state would send two top citizens to the United States Senate, where they would work with their peers to craft laws for the nation. The House would then be required to cooperate to pass bills that might become the laws of the land. If a bill survived this cooperative and deliberative effort, it would be sent to the president, who could sign it into law or could wield his veto power to reject it. It should be noted that the presidential veto power is not absolute but can be overridden by the deliberative process of Congress. The President must also submit a list of reasons for his veto. At every turn, the Founders set up a system to encourage a slow and truly deliberative process.

The Electoral College was established to encourage the selection of a good president in just the same way. The selection process would bring together in a deliberative environment, in their respective states, trusted public leaders, who would discuss top candidates and settle upon the best available chief executive for the nation. Alexander Hamilton summarized this situation in *Federalist* 68 by saying that it was desirable that the selection be made by a group of top citizens "acting under circumstances favorable to deliberation, and to a judicious combination of all the reasons and inducements which were proper to govern their choice."[20]

If this state-by-state process failed to give any single candidate a majority of votes cast, a similar process was established for the House of Representatives. Votes in the House would not be distributed to individual members, however, but to states—each counting as a vital political community and having one vote. This contingent process would thereby be deliberative at two levels. First, members of each state delegation would have to meet together to resolve on one person on whom to bestow their single vote. This process would tend to work against more radical or fringe candidates and in favor of moderate and compromise choices because of the fear that any delegation that could not arrive at a single choice would be disenfranchised in the selection process. Second, that initial choice would occur with an eye toward the choices of the other states and the likely vote distribution in the House. If a single candidate still failed to garner a majority of the states in the House, all the state delegations would continue to meet until this complex process within and between the state delegations resolved itself into settling on a fit candidate for office. Throughout, the deliberative process in Congress would be informed by the results obtained from the state electors, as the Constitution required the House to make its choice from among the top five candidates submitted by the state electors.[21]

Whether the selection ended with the electors voting in the states or with the House of Representatives, the process was never designed to be quick and easy. It was to be decentralized, slow, and above all, deliberative. It would not be quick, clean, or without controversy. But the result would be a president that was more fit for office than one selected through a hastier and less thoughtful process.

Federalism

The democratization of American politics has spawned a general political culture that considers any deviation from the basic assumptions of mass democracy as illegitimate. In America—and now we have taken to exporting this doctrine around the world—no system must stand that is not clearly laid upon the foundation of "one man, one vote." Though critics conveniently forget about the U.S. Senate's violation of that principle in its very structure, the Electoral College is seen as illegitimate and undemocratic for its failure to conform to this tenet. Thus, almost all of the Electoral College's critics would replace it with a single national plebiscite consisting of an aggregation of individual votes from across the nation.

As I have tried to show above, the Founding Fathers had a more complex and rich understanding of democracy than do many of today's pundits and politicians. They were convinced it would not be conducive to our common good to confine the political system to a simple and single formula of direct democracy. Rather, they established a complex system anchored to the more solid and varied foundations of a federative republic. As James Madison explained so clearly in *Federalist* 39 (see Appendix II), our Constitution is like a table with one leg upon the national community of individuals, a second upon the states directly as vital political entities, and yet a third upon a compound bond between the two. The Constitution itself was ratified by the votes of the states as sovereign states, not by a national referendum. Indeed, the ratification process was so constructed as to forbid any majority of states from binding the minority who did not freely choose to enter the new compact. Representation in the lower house of Congress was to be distributed according to population on a roughly one-man, one-vote proportional basis. But in the Senate, the states would exist as equal political entities, no matter their size in geography or population. The central government would act with power to compel individuals directly, which would add another national element to the system, but the states were to retain considerable authority over most functions of government, which adds another federal aspect for balance.

Mirroring the system as a whole, the presidential selection process was to be compound—both national and federal. The distribution of electors would partly be based on population (representation in the House) and partly on the states as autonomous political units (representation in the Senate). The system would be fair to both large states and small states, more populated regions and more rural communities. The process of selecting electors would occur separately in each state (and the method was left up to the people of the states to choose), and these electors would meet and deliberate within their own states. If the vote of the electors failed to resolve upon a single candidate, the more directly elected House would choose the president; however, House members would vote as single state delegations, adding yet another federative balance.

Understanding the origins of the Electoral College reminds us of the great care the members of the Constitutional Convention took to create a system with broad and strong foundations sunk deep into the complex nature of the Union. Though we celebrate diversity in other fields, the trend in modern America is toward a homogenization of our public life. The attempt to reduce the selection of our presidents to simple national plebiscites is just one of the latest manifestations of the leveling wind of democratization, which has given the Supreme Court control over state legislative elections and which has pundits and academics preparing the way for a new "virtual" politics of Internet connections and mouse-click democracy.

Discouraging Demagoguery

The Founders realized that there was a tendency in democratic politics, a phenomenon recognized by Plato, for ambitious democratic politicians to resort to inflammatory, dangerous, and divisive rhetoric in order to win votes. And they realized that this was a particularly dangerous possibility with regard to the selection of a single national president. Under the tactic of "divide and conquer," an unscrupulous candidate could cause great disruption in the social fabric by seeking to exploit class, regional, religious, ethnic, and possibly even racial differences. Rather than creating "a more perfect union," the stated goal of our Constitution, such a candidate would encourage ignorance and dis-union, because in these he would find power and prestige.

Several years ago, former President Jimmy Carter opined that it was time for America to revive the term "demagogue" and to not shy away from calling those politicians that appeal to our baser instincts by that name. He was returning to an understanding of democratic politics that is closer to the American founding than is the general political trend in America. The Founders were steeped in the history of the republics of Rome and of the democracy of Athens. From ancient history they knew the power a skilled orator could have over a populace. And the twentieth century, of course, provided fresh examples in the form of Hitler in Germany, Stalin in the USSR, and innumerable "softer" demagogues in America and all over the world.

In anticipation of such men, the Founders established what Alexis de Tocqueville would later call "forms." They believed that demagoguery flourished when all power was vested in a single entity (whether that entity was a single person, a small group, or a simple majority of the population itself). So they created constitutional institutions and mechanisms that would channel and control passions, ambitions, and demagoguery into safe and possibly even useful avenues.

In *Federalist* 10, James Madison attempted to show that the new constitutional order provided a way to deal with the problem of factions, which he defines as "a number of citizens, whether amounting to a majority or minority of the whole, who are unified and actuated by some common impulse of passion, or of interest, adverse to the rights of other citizens, or to the permanent and aggregate interests of the community."[22] He here showed particular concern for factious political leaders and argued that the Founders wished to make it "more difficult for unworthy candidates to practice with success the vicious arts by which elections are too often carried."[23]

Alexander Hamilton made the point even more clearly by extending Madison's concern to the election of a president, saying that the Constitutional Convention desired "to afford as little opportunity as possible to tumult and disorder," and that the system was set up to limit the "heats and ferments, which might be communicated" to the people at large. He added, "Nothing was more to be desired than that every practicable obstacle should be opposed to cabal, intrigue, and corruption."[24]

In the age of the thirty-second commercial, the six-second sound bite, and the racial divisions evident in our latest election for president, the Electoral College reminds us that a direct national plebiscite may not be salutary. Will destructive demagogues be further encouraged? Will our political life as a nation be further coarsened and our divisions widened? These are among the important questions that are raised by the specter of the Electoral College's abolition.

Separation of Powers

In his *Notes on the State of Virginia*, Thomas Jefferson wrote, "One hundred and seventy-three despots would surely be as oppressive as one," in his argument that concentration of government power "in the same hands is precisely the definition of despotic government." James Madison would claim, "The accumulation of all powers, legislative, executive, and judiciary, in the same hands, whether of one, a few, or many, and whether hereditary, self-appointed, or elective, may justly be pronounced the very definition of tyranny."[25] Perhaps no other principle of the American Founding is better known today than this basic presumption in favor of divided and distributed power. Every schoolchild knows the three branches of government, and nightly on our news programs we are witness to the courtship rituals (and sometimes to what seem more like divorce proceedings) between the executive and legislative branches of government.

Power was first split by the Founders between the states and the federal government. Those limited powers explicitly ceded to the national government were then further divided between the legislative, judicial, and executive departments. Each of those departments would be composed of diverse people who would hold their offices under various conditions and for various lengths of time. Perhaps most importantly, because the most important question is always where ultimate power rests, the various institutions were to be peopled with men chosen from a variety of constituencies selecting under a variety of formulas.

Likewise, if things went as planned, the president would be the choice of concurrent and deliberative processes in various states. The electors would be selected specifically to meet, deliberate, and cast their ballots for president and then would promptly dissolve as a body. A temporary body such as this made it less likely that the electoral process could be tampered with and that some preexisting body could choose, and thereby control, the chief executive. The entire presidential electoral process reveals the Founders' notion that power ought to be distributed and diluted. And to the degree that our political culture and institutions become animated by a simple plebiscitary ethic—which we can see in the proliferation of polls, focus groups, and political consultants—the closer we come to the single national system of concentrated power nearly all the Founders feared.

The Rule of Law

Understanding the origins of the Electoral College also reminds us of the importance of the rule of law to the American political experiment. As I have already conceded, the Electoral College is not simple and efficient. But neither is sustainable free government. The simplest form of government might be the tyranny of an individual, but how far is that, really, from the tyranny of the majority in a simplistic majoritarian system?

Quite simply, to say that America is governed by the rule of law is to recount the old phrase that we are a nation of laws and not of men. We are not to be treated differently because of our race or class, justice should not be for sale, and offices are to be earned through legal means and not purchased with cash or favors. Similarly, no person is made president simply because of the cheer of a crowd or his standing in the Gallup poll. Rather, presidents are made according to constitutional principles, legal proceedings in the states, and an aggregation of concurrent majorities all over the nation.

In a perverse sort of way, it was almost fitting that the presidential election of 2000 ended with a decision of the United States Supreme Court. By bringing a halt to the nearly lawless process of counts and recounts with floating standards in select communities in Florida, the Supreme Court reminded us all that as long as the Electoral College survives, at least, our presidential elections will be governed by the rule of law and not of men. Not much more could be asked of any institution in a free society.

Chapter II

★

The Development and Democratization
of the Electoral College

ANDREW E. BUSCH

The Electoral College has served as the nation's mode of presidential selection for over two hundred years with remarkably little constitutional revision. Indeed, if one were to peruse a copy of the Constitution from 1789 and a copy from 2001, one would think that virtually nothing had changed. One would be wrong. Indeed, while the form of the Electoral College has remained largely unaltered constitutionally, its operation has changed dramatically. A new, and distinctly more democratic, wine has been poured into the old bottle.

ELECTORAL COLLEGE ORIGINS

Originally conceived, the Electoral College was a compromise in at least two senses. First, it was a practical compromise between large states and small states. The formula for allocation of electoral votes gave the more populous states more electoral votes than the less populous states (at least roughly speaking),[1] but gave less populous states more electoral votes than their population would warrant proportionately. This compromise—theoretically speaking, the compromise between the "national principle" and the "federal principle" discussed by James Madison in *Federalist* 39 (see Appendix II)—was an embodiment of Madison's "compound republic."[2] It has endured to this day.

The other accommodation was a compromise between congressional selection of the president, a plan that initially had the most support, and direct national election, which was offered as the chief alternative. The two principles in this debate might be described as the principles of representation and a more direct national majoritarian democracy. This point should not be overdrawn, since many delegates supported congressional selection for practical rather than theoretical reasons (it was much easier logistically than direct popular election), and because those supporting direct election never indicated their approval of a plebiscitary ethos like that later embraced by Woodrow Wilson and others as the foundation of the modern presidency. Indeed, the objective of the supporters of direct popular election was primarily to maintain presidential independence, and secondarily to reduce the danger of corruption and cabal, which they thought a possibility if the selection was carried out by a small group like Congress. Both sides believed in a presidency grounded ultimately (directly or indirectly) in the people, and both sides believed in representative, constitutional government.[3] Yet, in the end, the Electoral College emerged as a viable alternative precisely because it artfully blended the principle of representation with the principle of popular accountability. That compromise, unlike the one between large and small states, has been almost entirely undone, as the representative features of the Electoral College have been phased out (in substance if not in form) and its democratic features accentuated. Indeed, it can be argued that it is only the continued vitality of the first compromise that has kept the presidential selection system from becoming entirely plebiscitary or "democratic," in a simple, majoritarian sense.

States were granted by the Constitution complete discretion over the means of selecting and allocating electors; part of the compromise lay in the way constitutional provisions did not dictate the exact degree to which states would be guided by a representative model. As a result, a variety of methods were initially used. Some states allowed for the popular election of electors, although more vested that power in the state legislature. Of the states using popular election, half allocated their electors by a statewide winner-take-all rule; the other half chose their electors by districts. Scholars today debate the nature of the expectations of most of the Framers regarding the independence of electors, a debate fueled by the near-total lack of discussion by the Convention. Nevertheless, at a minimum, it is clear that the constitutional structure allowed for electors to be unpledged representatives of their states who would operate in the fashion of "trustees" free to exercise their best judgment, well-informed and well-respected men of their communities to whom the people would delegate the authority to make a reasoned choice for president. It is also clear that at least some Framers expected exactly that outcome and publicly established that expectation.[4] In any event, the fundamental assumption underlying the electoral system was that elections would take place in an environment free of the effects of political parties.

EVOLUTION OF THE ELECTORAL COLLEGE

That assumption of non-partisanship survived less than a decade, as the Jeffersonian Republicans and the Hamiltonian Federalists arose in opposition to each other, first in George Washington's cabinet, then in Congress, then throughout the country. The rise of parties was central to the subsequent democratization of the Electoral College and American politics more generally. Between 1800 and 1860, four important changes thoroughly altered the operation of the Electoral College. Of those four, three were extra-constitutional; only one took the form of a constitutional amendment.

First, as the parties institutionalized themselves somewhat and began offering presidential nominees to the nation, the temptation quickly became irresistible for electors to make known their presidential preference in advance. Lord Bryce would contend a century later that no part of the Founders' constitutional scheme "has so utterly belied their expectations" as the fate of the independent elector.[5] As early as 1792, candidates for elector pledged themselves to vice presidential aspirants John Adams or George Clinton. In 1796, the year of the first contested presidential election, open supporters of the presidential candidacies of John Adams and Thomas Jefferson competed for positions as electors. Indeed, when one of Pennsylvania's pledged Federalist electors switched and voted for Jefferson instead, an unhappy Federalist, writing to the *Gazette of the United States*, exclaimed, "What! Do I chuse Samuel Miles to determine for me whether John Adams or Thomas Jefferson shall be President? No! I chuse him to *act*, not to think!"[6]

By 1800, a mere 12 years after the first presidential election under the federal Constitution, the parties were developing and offering pledged slates of electors throughout the nation. The prospect that electors would be independent actors using their own judgment was dead.[7] In its place, pledged electors with partisan loyalties directly transmitted the presidential preference of the voters (either the electorate at large or state legislators) into an electoral outcome. In the colorful words of Lord Bryce, "The presidential electors have become a mere cog-wheel in the machine; a mere contrivance for giving effect to the decision of the people."[8] This development alone moved the electoral process significantly in the democratic, as opposed to representative, direction. It is a mark of how completely expectations have changed that electors who stray from their candidate commitment, like the hapless Samuel Miles, are known in modern parlance as "faithless electors," a breed eccentric at best, if not actually contemptible. As the years passed, an increasing number of states—the number is now roughly half—passed laws imposing penalties on "faithless electors." Indeed, three-fourths of states today do not even list the names of the electors on the ballot despite the fact that they—not the presidential candidates—are actually the recipients of the vote.[9]

Second, as the general ethos of democratization spread, more and more states adopted the mode of popular election of the electors. By the election of 1824, only one-fourth of states used their state legislatures to select electors. South Carolina was the last state to use the practice in 1860, but it had long since become something of an anachronism—no other state had done so since 1828. Consequently, when Florida's legislature seemed prepared in December 2000 to name electors, most Americans did not realize that its action was consistent not only with federal law and the Constitution but with a practice with deep roots in American political history. Instead, it was widely attacked for trespassing on the democratic remolding of the Electoral College.[10] Like the first change, this shift in practice was

accomplished entirely outside the Constitution, this time through
the agency of state law.

Third, in recognition of basic mathematical realities, by 1836
every one of the 25 states using the popular vote had specified that
their electoral votes be allocated on a statewide winner-take-all basis.
In other words, whichever candidate received the most votes in the
state would receive all of the state's electoral votes.[11] As Judith Best
explains, winner-take-all (sometimes called the "unit rule" or "general ticket" system) "spread because it was favorable to the majority
party in each state, and because those states that did not consolidate
their electoral power were believed to have less influence and less
strength in an election than those that did consolidate."[12] Once a
large enough number of states adopted winner-take-all, the rest had
to follow. Anything else would have represented a sort of "unilateral
disarmament." In one sense, this change—again, achieved by state
law—was a victory for federalism. States were not only the venues in
which election would be sought, but by giving their votes as a unit,
they reaffirmed their standing as political entities. At the same time,
winner-take-all can be seen as another move away from the original
representative conception of the Electoral College. That is, if winner-
take-all bolstered the federal principle of the Electoral College, it also
arguably enhanced democracy over representation. It was clearly linked
with the move away from state legislative selection. Furthermore, the
local man of knowledge and judgment, even if an occasional example
could survive the predominance of pledged electors, could hardly
survive statewide election. And, as Best pointed out, the parties—or
to be more precise, the majority party in each state—had the most to
gain by delivering the state's votes in a bloc. The two greatest surges

of movement toward statewide winner-take-all rules came during the party-building eras of Jefferson and Jackson.

It was the almost universal acceptance of the winner-take-all rule that has given the modern Electoral College much of its character, and that is nearly as much an object of criticism as the Electoral College itself among its detractors. Though these critics often scorn winner-take-all as "undemocratic"—by which they mean that it does not reflect the variation of voting preferences within a state—it is actually highly democratic in the most basic sense. Whoever gets the most votes in a state wins. There is no consolation prize for finishing second, just as the presidency itself is indivisible. (For a view of the trend toward popular winner-take-all and against legislative selection, see Table.)

Finally, one important constitutional adjustment was made in 1804, in the form of the Twelfth Amendment, to align the formal operation of the Electoral College with its actual operation. This adjustment, like many electoral reforms in American history, was a response to a specific procedural breakdown. The electoral crisis that occasioned this constitutional change came in 1800, in the election between Federalists John Adams and Charles Pinckney and Republicans Thomas Jefferson and Aaron Burr. Originally, the Constitution provided for each elector to cast two votes for president, at least one of which had to be for someone from a different state. The top vote-getter (presuming he had a majority of electoral votes) was elected president, while the second-place finisher became vice president. This system, workable enough in a non-partisan environment, began to show signs of stress in 1796 when it resulted in two increasingly bitter opponents, Adams and Jefferson, being teamed together as president and vice president. In 1800 the system produced chaos.

Table

Methods of Selection of Electors Used by State, 1789-1836

By Percentage of States

Year (n)	Popular/ At-Large	Popular/ District	Popular/ At-Large + District	State Legislature
1789 (11)	27%	27%	0%	64%
1792 (15)	20%	20%	0%	67%
1796 (16)	19%	31%	0%	63%
1800 (16)	13%	19%	0%	69%
1804 (17)	35%	24%	6%	35%
1808 (17)	35%	24%	0%	41%
1812 (18)	28%	22%	0%	50%
1816 (19)	37%	16%	0%	47%
1820 (24)	38%	17%	8%	38%
1824 (24)	50%	21%	4%	25%
1828 (24)	75%	13%	4%	8%
1832 (24)	92%	4%	0%	4%
1836 (26)	96%	0%	0%	4%

All figures are rounded. Figures may total more than 100% due to rounding. Figures from 1789, 1792, and 1796 total more than 100% because two states in 1789, one state in 1792, and two states in 1796 used a two-stage process in which the legislature represented the run-off stage after an initial round carried out by popular vote either statewide or by district. Such states were counted in each category that applied. Tennessee in 1796 and 1800, which used an indirect form of legislative selection, is counted in the state legislature category. In 1789, two states had not ratified the Constitution and did not participate in the presidential election; New York did establish a mode of legislative selection, but failed to actually appoint electors due to a disagreement between the state house and state senate. It is nevertheless counted as one of the states using legislative selection. (Source: *Congressional Quarterly's Guide to U.S. Elections* 1st ed. [Washington, D.C.: Congressional Quarterly, 1975], 202-205, 948-949.)

By this time, both parties nominated presidential-vice presidential tickets and ran organized slates of pledged electors throughout the country. Because Republican electors were pledged to both Jefferson (as the presidential candidate) and Burr (as the vice presidential candidate), when they voted, Jefferson and Burr received an equal number of electoral votes, throwing the election into the House of Representatives for the first time in U.S. history. (Anticipating this problem, one Federalist elector voted for Adams but not Pinckney.) The contingency election in the House became deadlocked: Republican Congressmen voted for Jefferson, while Federalists, out of spite and calculation, voted for Burr, who would not stand aside. Alexander Hamilton intervened with some Federalist members of the House on behalf of Jefferson (or more precisely, against Burr), but not until two weeks from the date constitutionally set for inauguration of the new president was the deadlock broken in Jefferson's favor on the 36th ballot of the House. Having endured a constitutional crisis that could easily have ended in civil strife, Americans amended the Constitution to prevent a repeat performance. The Twelfth Amendment separated the presidential vote cast by electors from the vice presidential vote. In essence, the Constitution had been revised not to impose or facilitate a change in the electoral system but rather to recognize the reality that party tickets and pledged electors had already become the new norm.

CONTROVERSY, THE ELECTORAL COLLEGE, AND REFORM

While the Twelfth Amendment was the only significant constitutional revision of the Electoral College in American history, the crisis of 1800 was hardly the only election in which critics questioned the operation of the electoral system. Two other breakdowns were notable, though in each case the political response to the "misfire" focused for the most part on more incremental legal revisions or changes in elements of the electoral system outside the Electoral College.

In 1824, a field of four candidates—Andrew Jackson, John Quincy Adams, Henry Clay, and William H. Crawford—split the electoral vote evenly enough that no candidate received the majority required by the Constitution. The contingency election in the House was therefore used again, resulting in the election of Adams despite Jackson's apparent lead in both the national popular vote and the electoral vote.[13] Jackson and his supporters attacked the process as illegitimate, claiming that Clay had thrown his support to Adams in the House as the result of a "corrupt bargain" that made Clay Secretary of State. Jackson himself called for abolition of the Electoral College.[14] The democratic reaction to 1824 undoubtedly contributed to the decline in the number of states using state legislative selection from six states in 1824 to only one by 1832. Most of the Jacksonian rage, however, was focused on the presidential nominating process. It was almost universally agreed that the congressional caucus—or "King Caucus," as it was derisively called—had outlived its usefulness.[15] To critics it was too closed and too undemocratic, and was, in any event, increasingly incapable of structuring voter choice. No one any longer accepted its decision, a fact witnessed by the emergence of four strong candidates despite the caucus's designation of one official nominee (Crawford). Consequently, the drive for further democratization of American politics and the associated rise of mass-based political parties found an outlet in nomination reforms that ended in the establishment of the national party conventions.

The second "misfire" occurred in 1876, an election so rife with problems that few blamed the Electoral College system itself for the outcome. Republican Rutherford B. Hayes trailed Democrat Samuel Tilden in the official national popular vote but defeated him in the

Electoral College by one vote. However, this election represented anything but a clear-cut example of the plurality-loser phenomenon. Rampant, organized voter fraud on both sides meant that the actual popular vote total was unknowable. In addition, three Southern states and Oregon submitted competing sets of electors each claiming to be the valid winner. Hayes gained his bare electoral vote majority not through the normal operation of the Electoral College but because a special national commission, consisting of eight Republicans and seven Democrats, awarded him all of the contested electors on a party-line vote. The commission was a necessary expedient to break a deadlock between the Democratic House, which was unwilling to see the Republican president of the Senate (that is, the vice president) open and count the electors' ballots, and the Republican Senate, which was unwilling to trigger the contingency election in the House.

Many Democrats were outraged by the commission's decision. As presidential scholar Paul F. Boller Jr. explains, "The *Cincinnati Enquirer* called it 'the monster fraud of the century,' the *New York Sun* put black borders on its pages to mourn the demise of democracy, and a Washington paper even suggested doing away with Hayes.... In the House of Representatives the Democrats passed a resolution over Republican opposition proclaiming that Tilden had been 'duly elected President of the United States'; and in eleven states Democrats began organizing 'Tilden-Hendricks Minute-Men' clubs, arming themselves with rifles, and shouting 'On to Washington!' and 'Tilden or blood!'"[16] Crisis was defused when Southern Democratic leaders reached a behind-the-scenes accommodation with Republicans, accepting the commission's decision in exchange for promises that Hayes would end military reconstruction in South Carolina and Louisiana, appoint a Southerner to his cabinet, and funnel some federal aid toward Dixie. Only two days before the scheduled inauguration day, Hayes was officially announced the winner by the president of the Senate. Altogether, 1876 made 2000 look quite tame.

As after 1800 and 1824, Americans attempted to avoid a repetition of the crisis of 1876 by modifying electoral procedures. As was the case after 1824, though, those modifications did not take the form of a constitutional revision of the Electoral College. Rather, in the aftermath of the Hayes-Tilden dispute, Congress passed statutory legislation in the form of the 1887 Electoral Count Act, which sought to clarify the procedures to be followed in the event of contested electors and to establish that electors officially certified by their states through December 12 were not subject to challenge in Congress. These provisions became part of the arcanae of electoral law and quickly sank from public view—until they suddenly emerged as crucial to the resolution of the 2000 vote dispute in Florida.[17]

Interestingly, the one other case in the nineteenth century of the plurality-loser phenomenon—indeed, the only unambiguous case before 2000—was readily accepted by most Americans. When Benjamin Harrison lost the popular vote to Grover Cleveland but won an electoral vote majority in 1888, there was no significant outcry from citizens against an "undemocratic" Electoral College. Cleveland's defeat foreshadowed Al Gore's 112 years later. Cleveland, like Gore, amassed his popular vote lead by piling up huge margins in a few states—in Cleveland's case the South, in Gore's case a few big urban states like California, New York, and Illinois—but losing by smaller margins in most other places. In any event, 1888 seemed to show that popular anguish over the circumstances of 1824 and 1876 had less to do with the Electoral College *per se* than with perceptions that unfairness or illegality had tainted an otherwise sound process.

In the twentieth century, the Electoral College experienced none of the wholesale changes of the first half of the previous century. The Twenty-third Amendment, ratified in 1961, allotted three electoral votes to the District of Columbia. The franchise was expanded through constitutional amendment and congressional legislation, further democratizing American politics but having no direct effect on the operation of the Electoral College. Very close elections, like those in 1960, 1968, and 1976, spurred calls for reform or replacement of the Electoral College; some scholars even make the argument that a correct reading of the popular vote returns in 1960 puts Richard Nixon into the category of a plurality-loser.[18] And two small states, Maine and Nebraska, deviated from the winner-take-all norm by opting for the allocation of only two electors at-large and the rest by congressional districts.[19] Otherwise, the system forged in the early 1800s by pledged electors, popular selection of electors, the winner-take-all rule, and the recognition of party tickets built into the Twelfth Amendment has remained fundamentally intact.

To be sure, this stability has not been the result of lack of opposition to the Electoral College. Since 1797, over 700 constitutional amendments have been proposed in Congress to alter or abolish the Electoral College, and opinion polls over the last fifty years have consistently shown a majority of Americans favoring alternatives like direct popular election. Such polls must be received with some skepticism, however, since Americans have little reason to give much thought to such constitutional questions in their day-to-day lives. It is difficult to imagine that an informed, strongly held, active, and durable popular consensus in favor of change would not have achieved success by now. In 1969, an amendment advocating direct popular election passed the House with votes to spare and even enjoyed the nominal support of President Nixon, but was killed in the Senate; in 1979 a similar amendment received 51 votes in the Senate—a majority, but far short of the necessary 67.[20]

The very survival of the Electoral College is an indication that Americans have continued to accept it, even if they might not have designed the presidential selection system that way from scratch. Furthermore, to the extent that the polls can be trusted on this issue, Americans have actually grown less enamored of abolition of the Electoral College over the last third of a century. After the 1968 election, Gallup reported that 81 percent of Americans supported replacing the Electoral College with direct popular election, a full 20 percentage points higher than similar polls reported after the election of 2000.[21]

RESULTS OF DEMOCRATIZATION

What has this democratization (and party-fication) of the Electoral College meant? Most obviously, it has meant that, rather than being grounded in the popular will in some abstract or highly indirect way, presidential selection is now made by a direct conveyance of the popular will through the medium of preprogrammed partisan electors. The compromise between representation and democracy has been significantly altered in favor of democracy. Academic critics continue to refer to the anti-popular premises of the Electoral College,[22] but it is no longer possible, if it ever was—and that is a matter of debate—to correctly consider the Electoral College a manifestation of "elitism."

This change has almost certainly contributed to the continued acceptance of the Electoral College by Americans. Indeed, it is probably no exaggeration to say that the ongoing legitimacy—and therefore the survival—of the Constitution's presidential selection system was dependent on this development. Consequently, the federal principle in presidential selection, still central to the Electoral College, has been safeguarded. In turn, the federal principle has exerted a continuing limitation on democratization, as the popular will is still measured on a state-by-state rather than national basis. The democratic evolution of the Electoral College has therefore been in the direction of a complex democracy of concurrent majorities, not a simple and undifferentiated national majority.

The relationship of the democratization of the Electoral College to presidential power is not as simple as it might seem. In an absolute sense, presidential power has been enhanced. It is difficult to imagine presidents routinely claiming a popular "mandate" under a more representative and less democratic operation of the Electoral College. On the other hand, if it is true that democratization saved the Electoral College in an increasingly democratic age, then it might be said to have restrained presidential power in a relative sense. The primary alternative, after all, has long been direct popular election, which would have even further bolstered presidential mandate claims.

As even strong opponents of the Electoral College acknowledge, the system has carried the nation "most of the way down the road to a choice of the president by all the people."[23] However, the democratization of the general election phase of the presidential election system cannot go much beyond the point where it stabilized a century-and-a-half ago. It would seem that no further movement can be made in this direction without either eliminating the Electoral College altogether or modifying it in ways that encroach, to a substantial extent, on the federal principle. The Constitution, however, contains a nearly insurmountable defense of that principle. There are only two roads to constitutional amendment, and both travel through the states, three-fourths of which have to agree with any amendment. Thus federalism itself has been, and will undoubtedly continue to be, a powerful obstacle against any attempt to undercut federalism.

Chapter III

Federalism, the States, and the Electoral College

JAMES R. STONER JR.

One of the most remarkable facts of the remarkable election of 2000 was how readily most Americans acquiesced in the tally of the Electoral College, whereby a man was elected president with a constitutional majority that did not accord with the aggregated popular vote. Go back a mere twenty-five or thirty years ago and read what was written about the Electoral College then, and you will find that the dominant opinion was that Americans would never accept election by the College of anyone other than the winner of the most votes at the polls nationwide.[1] "One person, one vote" remains the constitutional law of legislative reapportionment, but the people seem more loyal to the Constitution than to any simple theory of nationalist majoritarianism.

Perhaps it was that, in the weeks before the election, Democratic commentators had reconciled themselves to the possibility that Al Gore might win the Electoral College but lose in the popular count. Perhaps because all the attention during the post-election campaign was focused on recounts and lawsuits, and all the ire of Democratic partisans after the denouement was directed at the United States Supreme Court, the actual vote in the Electoral College was anticlimactic and complaints against the College for the moment seemed minor or moot. Perhaps enough citizens and opinion leaders have grown to appreciate and even adopt the arguments found in this volume. Perhaps Americans have, in that mix of good sense and cynicism that seems the spirit of the age, simply acquiesced in "the system," figuring the consequences satisfactory enough and the prospects for reform not worth the effort.

Despite the temporary calm, a principled defense of the Electoral College remains crucial. In the first place, there is the need to support the legitimacy of our institutions: it does the country little good to doubt that the people govern, or to think of the Constitution as an arbitrary set of rules, part of a "system" that does well by those clever enough to master its intricacies but thwarts simple justice. Moreover, anyone who wants to think responsibly about the measures of reform that are sure to be proposed as soon as passage seems politically feasible, or their mere proposal politically useful, will need more than inertia as an argument. To be sure, most commentators quickly notice that the odds are long against passage of an amendment to replace the College with a direct popular vote, since more states stand to lose their relative impact on the election than the thirteen it now takes to block a constitutional amendment. But the scenario suggested by law professor Sanford Levinson, asked by the *Chronicle of Higher Education* to imagine how the case of *Bush v. Gore* will appear in fifty years, is more serious than playful: after a few more elections where the popular vote loser wins or nearly wins the electoral vote, a popular president who finally wins will call a constitutional convention that, under pressure, not only scraps the Electoral College in favor of direct election but declares that the ratification of constitutional amendments will henceforth take place by direct popular vote. (After all, Levinson reminds us, the Constitution of 1787, written by the last federal convention, was ratified by its own specified procedure, overriding the legally established process then in place.)[2] That Al Gore's half-million-vote popular plurality would have translated into even fewer electoral votes than he actually received if the redistribution of congressional seats after the 2000 census had taken place before the 2000 election suggests that the Democratic Party might have at least a short-term interest in replacing the College, a point not lost upon several of that party's leading politicians or intellectual friends.[3] And it is inconceivable that Mr. Gore and his backers would have fought for the presidency so fiercely after the election had they not thought themselves on the moral high ground because they had amassed the most popular votes.

Able defenses of the Electoral College have tended to take either a pragmatic or a constitutionalist perspective. The array of alleged pragmatic advantages is impressive, and many are undoubtedly true. Some argue that the Electoral College ensures that small states get noticed in presidential elections; some claim that the winner-take-all choice of electors in the states only magnifies the importance of states containing major centers of population.[4] (Ironically, in the election of 2000, both were true, for George W. Bush needed every three- or four-vote state he got for his victory, while if Al Gore had won a few thousand more votes in Ohio—or of course a few hundred more in Florida—he would have won the College with a commanding lead and no contest.) In addition, the effect of funneling the popular vote through the College often turns relatively weak popular pluralities into decisive electoral victories. (This was the case in both of Bill Clinton's elections, in Woodrow Wilson's first, and Abraham Lincoln's.) The imperatives of the College discourage third parties and their consequent fragmentation of the electorate, frustrating the dream of every radical and stanching the historic blight that clings to many of the failed democracies of the last two hundred years. Since the vote in the College itself is public and certain, with popular balloting conducted state by state, the Electoral College avoids the chaos and danger—now readily imaginable—that would accompany a nationwide recount. And then there is the counsel that recalls the danger of unintended consequences which accompanies any reform.

The constitutionalist defense of the College links it with the other institutional arrangements of the federal government which check and balance the force of national majorities: the separation of powers, bicameralism, equal representation of the states in the Senate, an independent judiciary, the rule of law itself. No one, of course, is an originalist on this point, since the Electoral College quickly ceased to be an assembly of notables choosing the nation's best and became instead a conduit of party competition—though it might be noted that the first architects of the political parties were some of the Founding Fathers themselves. What the constitutionalist perspective clearly highlights is the really misleading character of what has been called for generations the "popular vote": if the popular rather than the constitutional majority had been thought decisive, some voters might well have voted differently, and the candidates surely would have campaigned differently, not ignoring a state, especially a populous state, once they determined the state's vote was committed for or against their campaign, or directing all television advertising to a national audience rather than to media markets in targeted states.[5] Indeed, to alter the College would undoubtedly mandate a change in the whole process of presidential selection, which from the first caucus to the last recount is focused on the individual states precisely because that is where electors are chosen and where they vote.

THE ELECTORAL COLLEGE AS A DEMOCRATIZING INSTITUTION

What is usually overlooked in defense of the Electoral College, and what is to my mind decisive, is that the College now functions as a profoundly *democratic* institution: historically it has been the engine that fueled the movement toward democracy on the federal level, while today it safeguards democracy where it is, and can be, most genuinely democratic, namely, in the states.

The historical point is widely known but seldom made. In 1800, when the liability of the original electoral system was discovered (ticket voting led to a tie between Jefferson and his vice presidential candidate, throwing the election to the House and precipitating the Twelfth Amendment; see Chapter II), only six of the sixteen states chose their electors by a system that included popular voting, most opting instead for a choice by the state legislatures. By 1824, there were twenty-four states, only six of which still allowed their legislatures to choose electors, and within a few years there was only South Carolina, which persisted in this practice until the Civil War.[6] The 1820s also saw the democratization of candidate selection, with the demise of nomination by caucuses in state legislatures and the rise of state nominating conventions. "King Caucus" in Congress likewise fell into disrepute, thanks to the failure of any of its candidates to win an Electoral College victory in 1824 and to Andrew Jackson's successful campaign to discredit the election of his opponent by the House as a "corrupt bargain," catapulting him to a decisive victory in 1828. The first national nominating conventions were held in the early 1830s, in time for Jackson's re-election.[7] Because the Electoral College is chosen by the states, the democratization of the choice of president in the age of Jefferson and Jackson, like the expansion of the franchise and popular election of governors and even judges, resulted entirely from state reforms. As happens so often in American history, the movement was national because the states moved in concert.

At the beginning of the twentieth century, another wave of democratization swept the states, establishing in many of them processes of direct democracy—such as the legislative initiative and referendum—to supplement if not replace representation. When the Seventeenth Amendment, ratified in 1913, took election of United States senators out of the hands of state legislatures and gave it directly to the people of the states, it ratified a practice already more or less developed in some of the states—the famous Lincoln-Douglas campaign for the Senate in 1858 was actually a campaign between two tickets for the Illinois state legislature—though the effect was to divorce state elections from federal politics. While modern expansion of the franchise to blacks, women, and the young has involved amendment to the federal Constitution, even these reforms were pioneered in states. And, embarrassing though it may be to friends of democracy, segregation and the disenfranchisement of blacks in the South in the first half of the twentieth century—two notably anti-democratic developments—took place not in spite of, but as a result of, majority rule.

Still, today the states are more democratic than the federal government. Even leaving aside democratic processes such as the initiative and the election of judges, which are of long standing in the states but unknown at the federal level, government in the states is more immediate and more accessible to the citizens, both voters and candidates for office. Local interests that despair of making their voices heard in Washington can more readily achieve representation in state legislatures and in municipal governments that are the creatures of the states. Political careers get started here, where television is not the only medium of communication and candidates can still campaign door-to-door. New populations get involved in local and state politics long before they make a mark on the national scene. This is no modern accident, but an essential element of the federal system altogether understood at the time of the Founding. Indeed, the most telling Anti-Federalist objection to the Constitution of 1787 was that the representative institutions it established would make impossible the reproduction in miniature of the demographics of the people that was common in the state legislatures.[8]

THE STATES AS POLITICAL COMMUNITIES

If state and local governments are necessarily closer and more accessible to the people, the concerns they oversee are often the most immediately important in people's lives: education, security of person and property, keeping the peace, and much else that entails not only the protection of individual liberty but the development of a common life. Of national politics most people are necessarily spectators, and it is no accident that they cluster into ideological coalitions, for their interests are typically distant and abstract. In the states, interests are immediate and concrete, and again it is no accident if the ideological labels that attach to the national parties often fail to predict the policies of their members in local government. It is one thing to be opposed in principle to abortion and quite another to foster the networks of support for family life that make child-bearing honored, attractive, and rewarding. It is one thing to endorse civil rights and quite another to foster genuine peace and understanding among populations that live side by side in distrust or hostility and form their opinions of one another on the basis of lived experience. It is one thing to be anti-tax or pro-labor, another to figure out how to encourage prosperity and to care for the streets and parks and schools and libraries of the community in which one lives. In the states, in short, one finds the real life of political communities, with all the struggle, disappointment, triumph, and complacency that demo-cratic politics entails.

Some measure of state autonomy is appreciated by observers at the national level. Liberals stress that the states can serve as laborato-ries to test new legislation; conservatives like the competition between them for investment and even for citizens, thinking this the real test of policy success. But the states are more than useful instruments: they are the political voice of the diverse moral communities bound together in the federal republic. In punishing crime, protecting life and property, promoting education, and fostering morality, the states naturally differ, according to their different circumstances, traditions, populations, and choices; some are more efficient than others, some more successful, some more just. Of course there are many things they leave for the federal government to do, especially concerning the provision of national defense, the regulation of an increasingly complex and integrated economy, and the protection of those rights that belong to American citizens no matter where they are. As the protection of individual rights abstracted from the particular communities that give them meaning has increasingly become the coin of public discourse in recent years, the federal claim has been expanded, and lest I be misunderstood, I hasten to endorse the value and importance of federal protection for legitimate rights. But community too is a good, and in some ways a very democratic good, and it is the states that remain vibrant self-governing communities, each with its own identity—and true to their diversity, some with a stronger sense of that identity than others. To those of us who do most of our business over the phone or the Internet and have to take a plane to see our friends, the states might seem an annoyance or an amusement, and we move among them indifferently. To the many Americans who do not belong to what might be called the federal class, who live their lives near their families or move somewhere and put down roots and stay, the states are most emphatically home.

By tallying votes for the highest office of the land by state, even giving each state a sort of bonus for being organized as a state, the Electoral College affirms the importance of these self-governing communities and helps secure their interest in self-government. We know this intuitively, as the whole process of presidential selection focuses national attention on the states and their distinctiveness. We are reminded of the tremendous diversity of our country as we watch the candidates move around the country for the caucuses and primaries, and then during the fall campaigns, learning again every four years something new about the coalitions that are patched together to support each set of contenders. Having to go to the people, not as an undifferentiated mass, but in their states, makes candidates aware of, if not always sympathetic to, the whole array of interests articulated principally at the local level but held by people whose votes they need. Of course campaigns for national office ought to focus on national issues and to feature candidates of national stature, and on the whole they do. But to elect the president in a national plebiscite would either suppress what is local or, as has already been the trend, nationalize local concerns, removing their governance away from communities and into the inevitably bureaucratic machinery of a central administration. Much more than did the Seventeenth Amendment, abolishing the Electoral College would diminish the states, treating them as mere vehicles of local administration, not guardians of something as fundamental as self-government. And every diminution of the states in an age of centralization portends further diminution, until equal representation in the Senate and the role of the states in ratifying amendments seem anomalous and indefensible, and the ancient, basic structure of our government is undone. The Electoral College, in other words, for all its uniqueness, in fact plays a critical role in binding together the complex articulation of diverse interests and mixed principles which characterizes, indeed is the glory of, the American constitutional order. Like that order as a whole, it is, in James Madison's words, "partly federal, and partly national," partly concerned with the broadest and most uniform interests of individuals, partly reflective of democratic communities in all their distinctiveness and pride.

To speak well of the states and their traditional place in the American constitutional order is to ensure one will be accused of taking a romantic view of things, out of line with a hard-headed recognition of the globalization of modern life and blind to the patterns of injustice associated in American history with states' rights and local prejudice. Though the romantic label is not one that in every context I would wish to eschew, there need be nothing romantic about drawing attention to the valuable role of the states. As many have noted, ours is an age of the devolution of power as well as globalization; indeed, the processes may go hand in hand, as the ready exchange of information makes knowledge more locally available and as trends towards utilitarian monotony spark an interest in what is independent and distinctive. That the states have been known to work injustice is not in itself an argument against them—so has the federal government, and, besides, the power to do wrong is an unavoidable concomitant of the power to do right. The danger of local prejudice was well known to the Framers of the Constitution, and they succeeded in creating institutions to counter-balance it, not all of them democratic. It is no accident that those who would minimize the place of the states typically make appeal to the least democratic institution of our whole system, the federal courts, and then object most strenuously when those courts protect the states.

In a televised speech to the nation in the midst of the storm of recounts and litigation in late November 2000, Vice President Gore began by saying, "Every four years there is one day when the people have their say." That's not the way it works in my state: We vote several times a year on different propositions, we elect representatives to different levels of government, including the United States Congress, in between the presidential years, and we come across many of them in our communities as we go about our daily lives. That's democracy, and compared to a scenario where all that matters is one vote among a hundred million in a plebiscite for a single ruler in a distant place, I think it's a pretty good thing. It isn't perfect, but neither are the people who run and rule, who pursue their ambitions and their interests, who promote their causes and their friends. Constitutional government and what we now call democracy are not for angels, the Founders of our government famously instructed us, nor did they suppose that we ourselves could live as gods.

Chapter IV

Moderating the Political Impulse

PAUL A. RAHE

Now that, for the first time in more than a century, we have had
it dramatically brought home to us that, under the present
system of selection,[1] a presidential candidate can fail to gain a plurality
in the popular election but nonetheless win a majority of the votes in
the Electoral College,[2] there will no doubt once again be an assault on
that venerable institution and a concerted attempt at its abolition on
the part of those who can barely conceal the contempt that they
harbor for our country and its remarkable constitutional tradition.
Even before the presidential election of 2000 had been decided,
thoughtless pundits, such as E. J. Dionne of the *Washington Post*, and
shameless demagogues, such as the Senator-elect from New York,
were already out in front. There would soon be others, many others—
and by no means just from within the ranks of the Democratic Party.
Over time, the numbers are likely further to grow.

The last serious attempt at abolition was concerted in the aftermath of George Wallace's impressive showing in the 1968 presidential election, which had reminded Americans of the ever-present pos-

sibility that the appearance of a third-party candidate might someday deny both of the major-party candidates a straightforward majority in the Electoral College and open the way for bargaining in the period before the electors' meeting for the casting of ballots—or even throw the decision into the House of Representatives. Even before this event, there had been considerable agitation on behalf of abolition.[3] The Subcommittee on Constitutional Amendments of the U. S. Senate Committee on the Judiciary had held hearings on the subject and had collected testimony in 1966. A year later, a blue-ribbon commission appointed by the American Bar Association had presented a report on the question, denouncing the Electoral College system as "archaic, undemocratic, complex, ambiguous, indirect, and dangerous," and proposing the direct popular election of the president with a proviso that there be a run-off between the top two contenders if no one secured 40 percent of the vote or more.[4]

As a consequence of the Wallace candidacy, this proposal soon garnered support not only from the American Bar Association itself but also from the AFL-CIO, the United Auto Workers, the International Ladies Garment Workers Union, the League of Women Voters, the United States Chamber of Commerce, the National Federation of Independent Business, and the National Small Business Association. Public opinion polls suggested that 80 percent of Americans supported it as well; and when Senator Quenton N. Burdick wrote to the nation's 8,000 state legislators, more than 90 percent of the 2,500 who tendered a response favored a reform of the Electoral College, and nearly 60 percent preferred directly electing the president.[5] Accordingly, in 1969, a resolution proposing an amendment along the lines suggested by the Bar Association's blue-ribbon commission was introduced in the House of Representatives, and, in September of that year, it passed by a margin of 339 to 70, well over the requisite two-thirds. In due course, a virtually identical proposal was introduced in the Senate by Senator Birch Bayh with sponsorship from 39 of his colleagues.

In August 1970, the Senate Committee on the Judiciary voted 11 to 6 to report this proposal out of committee for consideration by the Senate as a whole. On this occasion, the six dissenting members of the judiciary committee—James Eastland, John McClellan, Sam Ervin, Roman Hruska, Hiram Fong, and Strom Thurmond—displayed a salutary prejudice in favor of American tradition and, putting aside their partisan differences, spoke up eloquently in defense of our peculiar form of constitutional government.[6] It was largely due to their efforts that opponents of the amendment managed to prevent cloture and head off a Senate vote on the pertinent resolution.

The success of the dissenters' effort should give us occasion for reflection. Apart from old Strom, who is due to retire in 2002, and Kentucky's Mitch McConnell, we should ask ourselves, where, in either major party, is one to look for such curmudgeons now? Understanding of the institutional logic of our Constitution is today in short supply—in the academy, among the general populace, and not least among those sworn to uphold that Constitution.

That the Electoral College will now be subjected to assault is as unfortunate as it is inevitable. It is inevitable because of the populist instincts inherent in a political regime that traces authority to the consent of the people. In such a polity, anything that seems in any way to thwart the popular will is quite naturally taken as an affront. "One man, one vote" has been the touchstone of legitimacy since

1962, when, in *Baker v. Carr*, our misguided Supreme Court swept away the modest restraints on majoritarianism that various states had adopted in imitation of the federal Constitution's allocation of seats in the Senate.[7] As a consequence, the tail is now wagging the dog: we are, in effect, now being asked, as constitutional scholar Alexander Bickel put it in 1968, to "amend the Constitution to make it mean what the Supreme Court has said it means."[8]

Why, opponents of the Electoral College quite understandably ask, does this principle—"one man, one vote"—not apply to the most important of our elections? How can it be fair that the vote of a citizen in one state ultimately has more weight in determining the result of an election than the vote of a citizen in another state? Is it not intolerable, they say, that a candidate who wins a plurality of the popular vote in a given state receives not a part but all of its electoral votes? Is it not doubly intolerable that someone might win a popular majority in the requisite combination of states but lose the national popular vote?

Such an eventuality does seem positively undemocratic—and, of course, in a modest way it does depart from the principle announced in *Baker v. Carr*: the current method of selection presupposes that the choice of our chief magistrate should be made by the people in their capacity as citizens of the various states rather than by the people as citizens of the nation as a whole. The crucial question—never even raised, much less considered by those intent on fully nationalizing what has always been a partly national and partly federal function—is whether this ill-understood arrangement is not somehow of genuine advantage to the United States of America.[9]

It is, in fact, a grave misfortune that the Electoral College is once again in serious danger, for, as will become clear in the course of my argument, this ill-understood institution constitutes one of the mainstays of our polity.[10] As John F. Kennedy remarked on the floor of the Senate in 1956, "It is not only the unit vote for the Presidency we are talking about, but a whole solar system of governmental power. If it is proposed to change the balance of power of one of the elements of the system, it is necessary to consider the others."[11] This is especially obvious when one contemplates the character of our two-party system. To the degree that we have managed to conduct our political life over the past two centuries without excessive bitterness and violence, it is largely due to the manner in which the Electoral College shapes our regime and the loose-knit parties to which it gives rise.

THE INTENTION OF THE FRAMERS

Oddly enough, our good fortune in this particular is not due to clairvoyance on the part of the Framers of our Constitution.[12] To be sure, they understood perfectly well that an election depending on the vote of the states *qua* states would add to the significance of the states as such and thereby bolster the federal principle, and they did envisage the separate election of the president as a means by which to ensure his independence from Congress and thereby reinforce the separation of powers. A number of the Framers feared, quite rightly as it has turned out, that, if the states as autonomous, self-governing units were denied leverage within the national government, they would eventually be subjected to it and reduced to providing ancillary services on its behalf. Moreover, the republican experiments that had taken place in the states during and after the revolutionary war had taught the Framers a lesson—that an executive elected by the legislature would be its pawn and that an executive of this sort could not be trusted to be impartial in his execution of the laws.[13] Where James Madison and his colleagues at the federal Convention erred was in supposing that the Electoral College would guarantee that there would be a genuine two-stage election.

The delegates to the Constitutional Convention quite consciously rejected "one man, one vote" as the sole standard of legitimacy when they established corporate representation in the United States Senate for the states as states, and the American people endorsed this prudential qualification of the majoritarian doctrine when they ratified the Constitution. In similar fashion, the Framers and those who voted for ratification hoped that the Electoral College would modestly enhance the significance of the less populous states. Their main aim, however, was to make the presidency an obstacle to partisanship.[14]

Their expectation was that each state would elect by the means that it deemed most appropriate a cohort of local notables, holding no federal office, equal in number to its representation in the United States Senate and House of Representatives. These notables, distinguished among their fellow citizens by a reputation for public-spiritedness and prudence, would in turn journey to a convenient meeting place within the state to deliberate in common and cast their ballots in secret for two candidates—only one of whom could be a favorite son from their own state. Thereby, it was supposed, chiefly by means of the ballot each was required to cast for the favorite son of another state, they would choose for our country's presiding officer in a manner free from cabal, intrigue, and corruption a wise patriot of continental reputation able to transcend the new nation's regional divisions and the factional bickering that would inevitably, at times, afflict the two houses of Congress.[15] Of course, when there was no candidate of sufficient stature to command a majority of the ballots cast, the House of Representatives was to decide—but not with full freedom and not in the ordinary fashion with each member casting a single vote. Instead, the House was restricted to a consideration of the leading contenders, who were in effect nominated by the Electoral College,[16] and the congressmen from each state were to gather, deliberate among themselves, and, by majority vote within their state caucus, cast jointly the one ballot allotted for this purpose to their state. This complex process was designed to ensure the election of a distinguished individual, to insulate his elevation as much as possible from the ordinary operations of the existing political bodies, to obviate political bargaining, and thereby to render the new president independent of the other branches of government, both federal and state.

The Framers of the Constitution would have been appalled at the notion that over time the presidency would become an object of partisan ambition, that candidates for the Electoral College would be identified on the ballot as supporters of particular candidates or pass unmentioned altogether, that in some states the electors would be required by law to vote for the candidate to whom they were pledged, and that for all intents and purposes the President of the United States would be directly elected by the people. The more astute among them feared the political passions that would inevitably be stirred up by so dramatic a contest with so much at stake,[17] and they were arguably right to do so.

Our presidency is a lightning rod. It is not an accident that so many American presidents have been marked out for attempts at assassination; it is not an accident that, in the immediate aftermath of one of our presidential elections, there was a civil war. In 1800, Thomas Jefferson feared that his election as president would be followed by a Federalist coup d'etat. As he understood, where the dictates of justice are a bone of contention, as is nearly always the case to one degree or another in great national elections, anger is never far afield. This is especially so where the contest somehow concerns the character of the bonds of friendship that enable a people to speak of a state and nonetheless think it their home.

For the most part, however, we have been quite fortunate—more fortunate, for example, than the citizens of the republics that emerged in Latin America in the wake of the wars of the French Revolution, more fortunate than the citizens of the new republics that emerged in Africa and Asia in the first three decades after World War II. We have never suffered a coup d'etat, violence has been exceedingly rare, and we have generally conducted our affairs with a modicum of restraint, civility, and even good grace. Our good fortune may have something to do with our character as a people, but this character is to a considerable degree a product of the workings of our Constitution, and it is here that the Electoral College has exercised a profound influence unforeseen by the Framers and largely unnoticed since.

THE ELECTORAL COLLEGE AND OUR PARTY SYSTEM

Because of the Electoral College, presidential candidates and the parties that support them campaign in such a manner as to construct a constitutional, as opposed to a popular, majority. To be precise, they seek to win a majority of the votes in the Electoral College, and to construct this constitutional majority, they must secure a plurality of the popular vote in each of a group of disparate states that together are endowed with the necessary electoral votes. Rarely can this be accomplished by a candidate who fails to win a popular plurality and a near, if not clear, majority within the nation as a whole.[18] That this can happen, however, when the election is exceedingly close, everyone now knows.

The virtue of this complex system is that it inadvertently achieves something of what the Founding Fathers intended. The crucial fact is that it militates against petty factions and regional parties, which have little hope of placing one of their own in the presidency. Given the diversity of our country, this in turn dictates a modicum of moderation on the part of the presidential candidates and of the parties that support them.

These parties and their nominees must aim at the achievement of a national consensus. They must be competitive in an enormous variety of venues. Every four years, they must attempt to present a program and an argument to justify it that will attract support from a plurality of citizens in a great many distinct constituencies—each with its own peculiarities. This discourages religious bigotry and tempers ideologically charged partisanship. It encourages coalition-building and careful attention to the varying needs and concerns of exceedingly diverse groups. It promotes a politics of inclusion. A party may write off a particular state or even a region in a particular presidential election. Very, very rarely, however, can it afford to do so for long.[19] Given the fluidity of our politics, our parties generally strive to remain competitive everywhere.

Because of the Electoral College, no party intent on victory can afford to pour scorn on the Jews of New York, the Mormons of Utah, the Muslims of Michigan, the Catholics of Illinois, the Armenians of Massachusetts, or the evangelical Protestants of Oklahoma. No one can ignore the concerns of aboriginal Americans or those of hyphenated Americans—whether they trace their ancestry to Europe, Mexico, sub-Saharan Africa, Asia, or the Middle East. The American Jewish Congress understood what was at stake in 1969-1970 when it opposed the direct election of the president, and it is no accident that the National Association for the Advancement of Colored People (NAACP) treated the proposal under discussion that year as highly suspect and then forcefully joined the defenders of the Electoral College in 1977, when Senator Bayh, with strong support from President Jimmy Carter, once again pressed for its abolition.[20]

Congressman William L. Clay of Missouri knew what he was talking about when he told the Senate Judiciary Committee in 1970 that the "direct popular" election of the president "would promote and reward...factionalism and sectional movements" and that it would lead to "the demise of the two-party system" and thereby "inhibit the political influence" of his fellow African-Americans; and he was right when he then warned that, in its absence, this particular "minority vote would likely follow a separationist trend."[21] In 1977, Vernon E. Jordan Jr. made much the same argument, contending that the amendment proposed by Bayh would "open the door to the end of the two-party system," that it "would severely limit" African-American "political leverage in national elections," and that it "would ultimately mean formation of black parties voting along racial lines."[22] As these two men had over time come to recognize, the Electoral College as currently constituted confers on the African-Americans scattered throughout the various states—and holding the political balance in many of them—considerable influence within the political system as a whole.

WATERSHED ELECTIONS AND THEIR AFTERMATH

In normal times, the manner in which the Electoral College structures our national contests gives rise to an exceedingly fluid two-party system built upon tenuous compromises between ideological factions and special interests, which are forced at every turn to moderate their claims. Third parties emerge and then quickly sink into insignificance or even disappear altogether if they fail to dislodge one of the two major parties. For a time, they give voice to those who feel excluded, and they generally exercise influence by forcing one or both of the major parties to bid for their supporters. In the nineteenth century, such was the fate of the Anti-Masonic Party, of the Free Soil Party, of the Liberty Party, of the Know-Nothing Party, of the Mugwumps, and the Populist Party. Such was the fate in the twentieth century of Eugene V. Debs's Socialist Party, of Teddy Roosevelt's Bull Moose Party, of Robert La Follette's Progressive Party, of Strom Thurmond's States Rights Party, of George Wallace's American Independent Party, and of the Reform Party of Ross Perot. Such will certainly be the fate of Ralph Nader's Green Party before ere long. If the Electoral College does not eliminate partisanship, it certainly shapes it and reduces its ferocity. For the sake of effectiveness, in America, partisans of all stripes are required to moderate their partisanship.

Of course, none of this prevents watershed elections. From time to time, despite the moderating influence of the Electoral College, matters have come to a head, and our polity has generated great tidal waves of popular opinion. The elections of Thomas Jefferson in 1800, Andrew Jackson in 1828, Abraham Lincoln in 1860, William McKinley in 1896, Franklin Delano Roosevelt in 1932, and Ronald Reagan in 1980 have reflected or occasioned great political shifts. In the aftermath of such elections, once the significance of the pertinent election has been made clear, the normal pattern reasserts itself; and, to survive, members of the opposition are forced to adopt elements of the program of the majority party and to appeal to marginal members of the majority coalition in a desperate but often quite successful attempt to slow down or moderate the great shift then underway. Recent history nicely illustrates our propensities in this regard.

Conservative Republicans may not much like William Jefferson Clinton but there can be no doubt that, on the domestic front, he was, despite being a Democrat, the most effective Republican president of the second half of the twentieth century. At the outset, he demonstrated great political flexibility when he secured passage of the treaty establishing the North American Free Trade Association (NAFTA) on the terms negotiated by his Republican predecessor. To be sure, early in his first administration, he raised taxes, and he and his wife mounted a vigorous challenge to the Reaganite consensus in the sphere of health care—but these initiatives served only to secure something that no Republican since Dwight D. Eisenhower had achieved: the election of a Republican Congress. When, thereafter, he surrendered more fully to the *Zeitgeist*, Clinton agreed to welfare reform and a dramatic reduction in capital gains taxation. Only by embracing that mainstay of the fiscal conservatives—a substantial, staged reduction in the national debt—have he and his fellow Democrats been been able to stave off the enactment of other elements of Ronald Reagan's domestic program.

Even then, had his administration not been beset by scandals, had Clinton not subjected himself to impeachment for perjury and obstruction of justice, had he not found it necessary to fall back for support on the liberal stalwarts within his own party, this highly malleable president might well have gone much further in promoting international free trade and in implementing other Reaganite reforms. The watershed election of 1980 determines our agenda to this day: the proponents of punitive taxation, the opponents of school choice, the admirers of our ethnic spoils system, the advocates of infanticide, and those hostile to the partial privatization of Social Security were on the defensive in the Clinton years, and they still are. Most of the time, in American politics, the question under discussion is less the direction of reform than the pace. Our institutions are admirably flexible: they discourage sharp differences and promote compromise but never entirely rule out seismic political shifts.

Only once in American history has the Electoral College spectacularly failed to secure the degree of national consensus requisite if we are to live peacefully alongside one another. Only once have we elected a president on a strictly regional basis. It is no accident that the election of 1860 was the most bitterly fought electoral contest in our entire history. Nor is it fortuitous that civil war followed the dissolution of the old Democratic Party and Lincoln's victory in an election in which his name was not even on the ballot in ten states. The Electoral College is remarkably salutary but it is not a cure-all. It managed for many years to delay a reckoning on the terrible question of slavery and to force on the contending parties compromise after compromise—but in the end, it could not prevent that reckoning. Nothing could.

DIRECT ELECTION

In the absence of the Electoral College, if all else were left unchanged, presidential candidates would aim at putting together for themselves a national plurality without regard to geography, and they would, therefore, ignore the less populous states and, in devising their programs, pay much less attention to the remarkable religious, ethnic, and cultural diversity that has always been the distinctive feature of our nation. As our parties then became internally more homogeneous, our politics would gradually become more ideologically charged, and there would be many fewer states and localities in which there was genuine electoral competition.

The losers in the great struggles that would then ensue would become embittered. Insofar as they were excluded from all influence and treated with undisguised contempt, they would become disaffected, even hostile to the nation—and perfect dupes for its enemies. The political struggle that took place in France during, and for a great many years after, the French Revolution became so bitter under the Third Republic that, in the mid-1930s, many a French patriot entertained the thought that it might be better to be ruled by Adolf Hitler than by the socialist Léon Blum.

In the United States, in the absence of the Electoral College, as partisanship gained in ferocity there would be a dramatic increase in voter fraud—as parties inflated their vote in each and every one of the localities they controlled in order to secure a plurality nationally. The squalid struggle over the recount by hand that took place in Florida during the last presidential election would be re-enacted repeatedly in a great many places.[23]

Before long, the two-party system would collapse—for there would no longer be any need to negotiate the myriad of deals that enable a party to construct an Electoral College majority. Small parties founded by the disaffected would become a permanent feature of our political landscape, for they could then hope, as they cannot seriously hope now, to extend their reach far enough to secure a plurality of the presidential vote in a multi-party conflict. As Arthur Schlesinger Jr. has warned, the direct election of the president

> would provide a potent incentive to single-issue zealots, freelance media adventurers, and eccentric billionaires to jump into presidential contests. Accumulating votes from state to state—impossible under the Electoral College system—splinter parties would have a new salience in the political process. We can expect an outpouring of such parties—green parties, senior citizen parties, anti-immigration parties, right-to-life parties, pro-choice parties, anti-gun-control parties, homosexual rights parties, prohibition parties and so on down the single-issue line. The encouragement of multiple parties would be a further blow to a party structure already enfeebled by passage into the electronic age.[24]

We might, of course, try to head off some of these difficulties in the manner proposed in 1969–70 and again in 1977: by staging a run-off between the top two vote-getters. This would, however, serve only to give further encouragement to voter fraud at the local level, for each party would be all the more intent on catapulting its candidate into the final round of the election. Moreover, as political scientist Nelson Polsby observed at the time that the run-off was under consideration, "The temptation under a direct election system would be strong for all manner of demagogues and statesmen—whoever can raise the money—to run, whether sectional candidates or movie idols with widely scattered following to appeal directly to the people. So there would be a high probability that...the run-off would be the true election, and the initial election would look a bit like the start of the Boston Marathon with its motley crowd of contestants."[25]

Between the first and second rounds, to be sure, deals would be cut between the surviving candidates and those who had fallen by the wayside—but these would have the appearance, and quite likely the substance, of corrupt bargains. Requiring, as they would, a naked abandonment of principle for the sake of political advantage, they would foster a profound cynicism concerning the political process while only enhancing the ferocity of the struggle for office and honor.

As Senators Robert P. Griffin and Joseph D. Tydings observed in 1970, in announcing their opposition to the run-off scheme, "Concessions wrung from major party candidates either before or after the first election would be made in a heated atmosphere conducive to the creation of public distrust. Given the fact that bargaining before the runoff election would take place under conditions of division and disappointment, cynical political moves might in themselves lead to a crisis of respect and legitimacy in the selection of the President." This would be doubly true, they added, "where the runner-up in the initial contest wins the runoff by wooing third-party support. In such a case, the question of legitimacy is sharpened even further if the turnout in the second election is substantially lower than in the first election."[26]

THE DISTRICT PLAN

There are, of course, alternative proposals, and there is an argument to be made on behalf of each. We might, for example, adopt a constitutional amendment retaining the Electoral College system and reforming it along the lines suggested by South Carolina Congressman George McDuffie in 1825 by creating electoral districts in each state equal in number to the state's representation in the federal Senate and House.[27] Alternatively, individual states might imitate Maine and Nebraska, allocating one electoral vote to each congressional district while reserving two additional votes for the candidate who wins the state overall. As historian Jack Rakove has observed,

> The winner-take-all rule might make sense if states really embodied coherent, unified interests and communities, but of course they do not. What does Chicago share with Galena, except that both are in Illinois; Palo Alto with Lodi in California; Northern Virginia with Madison's home in Orange County; or Hamilton, N.Y., with Alexander Hamilton's old haunts in lower Manhattan? States have no interest, as states, in the election of a president, only citizens do, and the vote of a citizen in Coeur d'Alene should count equally with one in Detroit.[28]

To this argument, one can add that the proposal advanced by McGuffie and the Maine-Nebraska model would have two advantages: they would discourage voter fraud in party strongholds by quarantining the pertinent districts,[29] and they would sustain the two-party system. Moreover, they really would dramatically reduce the chance that a candidate would win the popular vote nationwide while losing in the Electoral College. The trouble is that they would also embitter our politics, promote extremism within the two parties, and subvert the separation of powers.

To begin with, every ten years, in each and every state, there would be an even fiercer battle than now takes place to create gerrymandered districts favorable to one party or the other, and the party in control of the presidency would have an even greater motive for rigging the census than it has today. Moreover, once the gerrymandering had occurred, presidential candidates would have far less need than they have now to extend their reach and seek votes from members of insular minorities generally loyal to the other party—for the latter would quite often be concentrated, as they are now, in electoral districts that one party or the other would have no hope of carrying. Not many more electoral districts would be seriously contested than are congressional districts today, and only in this handful of districts would the presidential contenders strive mightily to eke out a plurality. Only in these districts would both contenders pay attention to the concerns of minority groups. Only there would citizens have a serious reason to vote. Such an arrangement would promote an even greater cynicism about the political process than now exists; it would intensify partisanship while eliminating most of the disincentives that now encourage our political parties to seek the middle ground; and it would promote all-too-close a connection between the election of the president and the election of the House of Representatives.

Strangely enough, then, Rakove has it backwards: the winner-take-all rule makes sense and promotes political moderation precisely because the states tend to be ethnically, religiously, and socially diverse and, in this sense, very rarely embody coherent, unified interests and communities. Because of the winner-take-all rule, candidates must concern themselves with Galena as well as with Chicago, with Lodi as well as with Palo Alto, with Orange County as well as with northern Virginia, and with lower Manhattan as well as with Hamilton, New York. In their quest to secure a plurality of the votes cast within a great variety of states, candidates must avoid unnecessary antagonism, and they must be sensitive to the needs and concerns of an enormous variety of citizens.

Moreover, as James Stoner argues in Chapter III, each of the states does, in fact, form a coherent and unified interest and community with regard to one highly pertinent particular: each is self-governing, and the citizens within each state have a stake in the defense of their local autonomy. Galena and Chicago are, indeed, both in Illinois—and Palo Alto and Lodi are both in California, just as lower Manhattan and Hamilton are in New York. These links matter a great deal. Only a radical nationalist, blind to the need for vigorous government on the local level and intent on consolidating power and influence in our nation's capital, could seriously argue that states, as states, have no interest in the election of a president. If they are to be anything more than instruments of national policy, the states must be capable of exercising leverage within the federal system.

The adoption of the Seventeenth Amendment, providing for direct election of senators where the original Constitution had provided for their election by the state legislatures, dealt federalism a near-fatal blow by entirely divorcing representation within the federal legislature from the interests of the states as self-governing corporations.[30] Repeal of the winner-take-all rule would only serve further to increase the quite severe damage already inflicted on the federal element within a polity that, James Madison quite rightly argued, was intended to be "partly federal, and partly national."[31]

THE BONUS PLAN

There is at least one other proposal under consideration, and at first glance it might seem attractive. In the late 1970s, the Twentieth Century Fund appointed to its Task Force on Reform of the Presidential Election Process a collection of historians, political scientists, journalists, and political practitioners—including Richard Rovere, Jules Witcover, Jeane Kirkpatrick, Stephen Hess, Patrick Caddell, Thomas Cronin, John Sears, Arthur Schlesinger Jr., and other figures less well-known—and, in 1978, this gathering of the great and good suggested yet another plan. Mindful of the stabilizing influence of the two-party system, they urged that the Electoral College be retained, and, persuaded that it was intolerable that we be saddled with a president denied democratic (as opposed to mere constitutional) legitimacy, they suggested that the winner of the popular vote nationwide be awarded an additional 102 electors, two for each state and two for the District of Columbia. "With an automatic 102 electoral votes," Schlesinger explains,

> the popular-vote winner would almost certainly win the Electoral College. The national bonus plan would balance the existing federal bonus—the two electoral votes conferred by the Constitution on each state—and would preserve both the constitutional and practical role of the states in the presidential election process. The plan, by encouraging parties to maximize their vote in states they have no hope of winning, would stimulate turnout, reinvigorate state parties, enhance voter equality, and contribute to the vitality of federalism.[32]

If the so-called bonus plan were as attractive as Schlesinger makes it out to be, it would, indeed, be worthy of consideration. If truth be told, however, its only advantage would be that it would further reduce the already small chance that a presidential candidate would lose the popular vote but nonetheless win an Electoral College majority.

To achieve this modest advantage, one would not only stimulate turnout and reinvigorate state parties but promote voter fraud on a very grand scale—for the bonus plan would give these reinvigorated state parties every incentive to turn out not only the living but those deceased, not only local residents but those who have long ago relocated elsewhere, not only citizens but illegal aliens, not only the law-abiding but convicted felons. This problem—which is quite serious already in venues as disparate as Newark, New Jersey; Detroit, Michigan; Philadelphia, Pennsylvania; Dade County, Florida; and, of course, Cook County, Illinois—would be made much, much worse.

Moreover, the bonus plan would not contribute to the vitality of federalism: it would sap it. This it would do by reducing the incentives for inclusion that now exist. Presidential candidates would still pay some attention to the less populous states, but they would be far more concerned with maximizing their vote in the party strongholds. When time and money are limited, candidates will be far less focused on eking out a victory by putting together a patchwork of states offering no more than twenty electoral votes apiece than with securing the 102 votes awarded the winner of a plurality of the national popular vote. The bonus plan may be preferable to direct election, but it would do great damage nonetheless.

OUR CONSTITUTIONAL TRADITION

In April 1970, when constitutional scholar Charles Black testified before the Senate Committee on the Judiciary, he prefaced his remarks with the observation that, when he spoke to students from abroad, he generally told them that, in America,

> we have in fact only one antiquity that is worth your attention. That is the Constitution of the United States. It was put into effect when Napoleon Bonaparte was a young comer. And as the other countries of the world, almost without exception, have rolled through one constitutional revolution after another, this thing has stood there in substantially its present form, has accommodated a whole continent and now reached out to the islands of the Pacific and brought them into a political structure of obvious solidity and strength. It is our antiquity. It is what we have to show you instead of the cathedral at Chartres.

Black admitted that he entertained a "bias" in favor of his country's constitution. "I approach this question," he acknowledged, "with the feeling, which I believe to be validated historically, as well as any can be, that the Constitution of the United States is an almost miraculously successful document, and that any change in its structure is to be approached with every presumption against it."

Black acknowledged that he could not prove beyond a reasonable doubt that instituting the direct election of the president would do irreparable damage to the political system. "These are prophecies," he admitted. "We do not know why this constitution has lasted so well. We do not know for sure wherein the strength lies, what it is that has given it such durability through so many troubles." It was his "hunch," however, "that this strength is somehow connected with the federal system," and he was persuaded that the abolition of the Electoral College would subvert that system. For this reason, he regarded the proposed reform as dangerous. If the amendment then under consideration were to be adopted, he warned, it would be "the most deeply radical amendment" ever to enter "the Constitution of the United States, looking on that Constitution in its bare bones aspect." He shuddered at the prospect that its proponents would succeed.[33]

Charles Black's testimony should give us pause. Whatever we may think of the Electoral College when we ponder this arcane institution in isolation, the political system within which it plays so prominent a role has been successful in a manner that merits on our part genuine awe. To tinker with that system for no good reason, simply because we find one element within it incomprehensible, would be to confer on our powers of rational comprehension a measure of trust exceeding that which has been generated in us by the visible and quite exceptional success of our political institutions over a great many generations. It was Black's suggestion that we be more modest in our assessment of the profundity of our understanding and more respectful of what can be inferred from the brute fact that our institutions, mysterious though they may seem, have withstood the test of time. This suggestion we would be well advised to embrace.

It is, in fact, high time that political observers and practitioners in this country abandon cheap, populist sloganeering and pause to reflect soberly and in depth on the consequences of what they propose to do. As the argument advanced herein should make clear, the Electoral College as currently established is one of the linchpins of our constitutional system. Despite its obvious but modest shortcomings, it has served us for more than two centuries exceedingly well. We would be fools to cast it away.

Those who love this country and are proud of its remarkable tradition of moderation, toleration, and inclusiveness, whatever their current political orientation, should put aside their other differences and unite, as a stalwart but constitutionally sufficient minority did in the Senate three decades ago, in that honorable tradition's dogged defense.

[An early, much abbreviated version of this essay appeared in The American Spectator Online *on November 14, 2000. It is reprinted here with permission.]*

Chapter V

✫

The Electoral College and the Future of American Political Parties

MICHAEL BARONE

"I used to favor abolishing the Electoral College," says Congressman John Dingell. "And then I changed my mind." Why? "Because the Electoral College tends to preserve the two-party system." Congressman Dingell speaks from a vantage point closer to the Framers of the Constitution than most of us: he is the senior member of the House of Representatives, so senior that the second most senior member of the House once served on his staff; he won a special election in 1955 to succeed his father, who was first elected to the House in 1932; he served as a page in the House in 1937, and so has a personal acquaintance with the chamber that spans 64 years. But despite his relative closeness to the Framers, it is beyond gainsaying that the Framers would not have agreed with his reason for supporting the Electoral College they established.

ORIGINS OF THE TWO-PARTY SYSTEM

For the Framers abhorred political parties, and party systems, and indeed continued to voice their abhorrence even as they created a two-party system in the 1790s. That system was created because the infant United States was faced with choosing between sides in a world war that raged from 1792 almost without interruption until 1815 between monarchical Britain and revolutionary France, the only foreign war in which Americans were about evenly split between sympathizers with one side and sympathizers with the other.

When that war was over, the first two-party system had effectively disappeared. But 20 years later, another emerged. And ever since, American politics has been mostly a competition between, for 20 years, Democrats and Whigs, and then, for 150 more years, Democrats and Republicans. The one time the two-party system broke down, in 1860, the result was civil war. The Framers did not intend it, did not want it, sought to prevent it: but a system which has helped to ensure the successful operation of the constitutional regime the Framers established must have something to say for itself.

What it has to say, in my opinion, is this. It forces politicians in a continental republic, with vast differences in cultural attitudes and economic circumstances, to come up with some combination of public policies that is capable of winning the approval of 50 percent of the people. It restrains the fissiparous tendencies of political ideologues and idealists, who seek to impose their will on a majority of those who reject their views. It prevents situations like that which afflicted the republic of Chile in 1970, when the winner of a 36 percent plurality in a three-way election won control of the government though most of the 64 percent who did not vote for him found him unacceptable; the result was a violent overthrow of the president, and the establishment of a dictatorship for more than a dozen years.

When parties have an incentive to win 50-plus percent of the vote, they also have an incentive to moderate regional enthusiasms, to compromise ideological principles, and to unite voting blocs with very different cultural backgrounds and attitudes and very different economic interests and goals. Without this, it is very hard to govern acceptably a republic that is continental in expanse and variegated in culture and ethnicity. In other words, there are powerful reasons, reasons that perhaps might even have proved attractive to the Framers if they had contemplated them, to prefer a two-party system to one which allows the proliferation of parties based on regional, ethnic, economic, or ideological factors.

BULWARKS OF THE SYSTEM

Yet there are only two institutional bulwarks of the two-party system in the United States today. One is purely statutory, and could be wiped out by Congress tomorrow: the single-member congressional district. It was not until the 1970s that Congress passed a law requiring that each district could elect only one member; before that, North Dakota elected two congressmen-at-large, and other states could have chosen that method as well. Indeed, it could still happen: if a state loses House seats in the decennial apportionment and no redistricting plan is enacted by the state or imposed by a court, all the House members must be elected at large, as happened in 1932 for the 13 House members elected in Missouri, the nine elected by Kentucky, Minnesota, and Virginia, and the two elected by North Dakota: 42 of 435 members. (And there is nothing constitutional about 435: the limit is the product of statutes passed by Congress since 1911, and could be changed at any time, though no one today proposes that.)

Single-member districts work powerfully against third parties and independents, because it is very hard to create confidence that third parties can be competitive in winning control of the House. There is a test case on this. The Progressive party ran candidates in many districts in 1912 and 1914, but elected very few. By 1918 the Progressive party had pretty well disappeared. Third parties have continued to run congressional candidates here and there, and very occasionally one wins. But these are usually parties with strictly local appeal, incapable of winning in more than a few districts. Also, Independent candidates are sometimes elected. But most of them are known to be reliable supporters of one major party or the other, like the two Independents in the House today: Vermont's Bernie Sanders votes and caucuses with the Democrats; Virginia's Virgil Goode votes and caucuses with the Republicans.

But the obstacles to third parties attaining the critical mass needed to compete on equal terms with the major parties in legislative elections are too great to overcome. The failure of Jesse Ventura's Reform party candidates to make any headway in election to the Minnesota legislature, despite Ventura's high poll ratings, shows how the single-member district is a powerful institutional support of the two-party system. Hence third parties tend to fade away, and political competition occurs again within the template of the two-party system.

The other great institutional support of the two-party system is constitutional: the Electoral College. Some contend the Framers expected that the Electoral College would be made up of local notables, who would ordinarily vote for prominent state or regional leaders, and that the House of Representatives would then choose among them. But it was clear by 1796 and 1800 that there would be national parties who would choose national nominees, and that continued to be the case after the demise of the Federalist party, when the single major party, the Republican-Democrats, chose their nominees in a congressional caucus. After that system broke down in 1824, competition between two national parties promptly reappeared. The Electoral College became the scoreboard that determined the winner of the contest between these two parties.

That works powerfully against third parties. Because all the electoral votes of each state are cast for the winner of a plurality of the popular vote, there is a powerful argument in almost every presidential election against voting for a third-party candidate: Don't waste your vote.

To be sure, third parties have occasionally become a factor in presidential politics, disastrously in 1860. When a third candidate wins the support of a critical mass of voters, enough to make him roughly equal with at least one of the major party candidates, the don't-waste-your-vote argument becomes much weaker. Or it turns against one of the major party nominees, as in 1912, when Theodore Roosevelt as the Progressive party nominee overshadowed the Republican incumbent, William Howard Taft. But that is the one case in 170 years in which that has happened.

More often, a third-party candidacy splits the apparently dominant party and shows the non-dominant party how to expand its constituency. Thus, in 1924 Progressive party nominee Robert LaFollette, a Republican senator for 20 years, split the Republicans, though not enough to deny them the presidency. But within a decade Democratic President Franklin Roosevelt adopted enough of the Progressive program to win over its constituency. To the existing Democratic base in the Solid South and the big cities of the North he added the Upper Midwest and Western progressives, and made the Democrats a majority party. Similarly, in 1968, George Wallace's candidacy won the votes of many former Democrats in the Deep South, and the Democrats lost the presidency. But Republican Presidents Richard Nixon and Ronald Reagan appealed to these same southern conservatives and made them an integral part of their Republican majorities.

In the 1990s two potential third-party candidates achieved a critical mass of support in the polls, but not in actual elections. In the spring of 1992 Ross Perot actually led in polls against George Bush and Bill Clinton. But Perot squandered his chance to win by, bizarrely, withdrawing from the race on July 16 and then, even more bizarrely, reentering the race on October 1. In the fall of 1995, Colin Powell led in polls against Bill Clinton and Bob Dole and other possible Republican nominees. But Powell declared that he was a Republican and, a little later, said he would not run for president at all.

No one can be sure what would have happened if Perot had not withdrawn or Powell had run; it is possible that one or both might have been elected. Thus we cannot say that the Electoral College totally prevents third-party candidates from winning. But the Perot and Powell examples, and that of Theodore Roosevelt, show that only a very few possible third-party candidates can achieve critical mass. Such candidates must be known nationwide. Such candidates must have an appeal that crosses regional lines: LaFollette and Wallace failed to become nationally competitive candidates because one could be competitive for electoral votes only in the Upper Midwest and

West and the other could be competitive for electoral votes only in the South. Such candidates must be capable of drawing votes from the usual constituencies of both of the major political parties: Theodore Roosevelt failed to be competitive with Woodrow Wilson because almost all his votes came from Republicans.

There are likely to be few such candidates. And in their absence, the Electoral College continues to discourage voters from casting votes for third-party candidates and to give the major parties an incentive to amass coalitions as broad as possible. For those who favor proportional representation or wish for a proliferation of parties, that is an unfortunate result. They argue that democracy works best when voters can choose a candidate with almost exactly the same set of views as their own. Then those parties can negotiate and make public policy. That argument is obviously stronger in a parliamentary system, where adjustments can easily be made in the makeup of the executive.

But in a presidential system, in which the winner of the electoral votes holds 100 percent of the executive for a set term, such adjustments are difficult if not impossible. Electing the president by popular vote would encourage the creation of more parties and the proliferation of third-, fourth-, and fifth-party candidates. It would give strength to strategists in the major parties who want to rely on the parties' core constituencies to achieve a plurality victory. The result would be more governments unacceptable to a majority of voters. In a continental and economically and culturally diverse republic, that would be a recipe for disaster.

Our two major parties may be awkward beasts, ideologically incoherent much of the time, deeply divided within themselves on occasion, perceptibly different in different regions. But they have proved to be the best mechanisms for achieving acceptable results in the republican framework erected by the Framers. Keeping the Electoral College will tend to keep our two major parties strong, and capable of presenting choices acceptable to a majority of Americans.

Chapter VI

The Electoral College and the Uniqueness of America

Daniel Patrick Moynihan

L et us start with the basic understanding that there is no fact more singular about our Constitution than its durability.[1] As a written constitution, it is the oldest in the world, save only for the medieval constitution of Iceland, which still persists in that island nation. No other large industrial, and certainly no continental, nation has anything like our experience of a sustained and stable government under a constitution basically unchanged from its original construction.

It is not widely understood how singular this history is, and I recall that one afternoon in the General Assembly Hall of the United Nations, in the course of a long debate on a not-altogether absorbing subject, I found myself looking at the two large scoreboards, as one might say, located in the front of Assembly Hall, on which the member nations are listed and where their votes are recorded.

I found myself asking how many of the 143—now 154—nation members of the U.N. had existed in 1914 and had not had their governments changed by force since 1914. It was not a great exercise to determine that in that great universe of nations, exactly seven met both those criteria—that they both existed in 1914 and had not had their form of government changed by force since.

There are some who might ascribe our good fortune to the insularity of the nation in its early years, and the size and strength of the nation in its later years. But I would say that, in no small measure, it has also been the result of the genius of the American Constitution and the way it has served this political community for almost two centuries.

THE AMERICAN FOUNDING

I would not disguise, at the outset, my sense of the measure before the Senate today, proposing the abolition of the Electoral College, to state that in the guise of perfecting an alleged weakness in the Constitution, it in fact proposes the most radical transformation in our political system that has ever been considered—a transformation so radical and so ominous, in my view, as to require of this body the most solemn, prolonged, and prayerful consideration, and in particular a consideration that will reach back to our beginnings, to learn how we built and how it came about that we built better than we knew.

At the base of Capitol Hill, just a few feet outside this chamber to the west, looking west past Schrader's great equestrian statue of Grant, past the Washington Monument, and on to French's seated Lincoln, is a bronze statue of John Marshall, also seated. It cannot altogether by chance be that these four men, defining the unity and tension of the active and contemplative in American public life, should be the only persons so honored on the central axis of the Mall. Nor is it chance that a marble tableau on the northeast face of the plinth of the Marshall statue depicts, in the allusive but plain language of our time, the scene of Minerva dictating the Constitution to young America.

This statue, erected in 1884, suggests that a century into our constitutional experience we had a live and vibrant sense that our Constitution was constructed by persons who had studied history and had come to what they viewed as a new and better understanding of what they thought might well be judged the principles of history.

It serves our purpose to look at the beginning with the Declaration of Independence and the "self-evident truths," as they were termed, by which the new nation sought to justify its revolution and its new form of government.

As the late Martin Diamond has reminded us, the political credo of the Founding Fathers, encapsulated in the words of Jefferson, was based upon the scientific and philosophic advances of the seventeenth and eighteenth centuries. The respect for human rights which constituted liberty as they understood it was not an idiosyncratic value of a remote group of Anglo-Saxons with no claim on any other political culture. It was not a tribal aspect of our inheritance. Rather, it was seen as the primary political good, of whose goodness any intelligent man would convince himself if he knew enough political science. In Diamond's words, "They regarded liberty as a modern idea, as the extraordinary achievement of seventeenth and eighteenth century political thought."

With that achievement in mind, George Washington, for example, said that Americans lived "in an epoch when the rights of mankind are better understood and more clearly defined than at any former period." This understanding and clarity were all part of the new "science of politics" to which Hamilton referred in the ninth *Federalist Paper*. I would cite that passage of Hamilton and his sense of how relevant it was. He noted that previous republics had had such stormy histories that republicanism had admittedly fallen somewhat into disrepute. This tendency, however, could be overcome, thanks to progress in political science. And Hamilton went on to say: "The science of politics, however, like most other sciences, has received great improvement. The efficacy of various principles is now well understood, which were either not known at all or imperfectly known to the ancients." Hamilton went on to cite as examples of "new discoveries" the various constitutional institutions with which we are now familiar: separation of powers, the system of checks and balances, representation of the people in the legislature, the independent judiciary, and so on.

It is important once again to remember that the Founding Fathers had learned from history—they had studied its principles—that liberty was not just a quality characteristic of the ancient peoples from which the American peoples sprang, but was a principle of government of which any person who would learn enough would persuade himself.

They recognized that republics in the past had been turbulent. They had all studied with great attention the history of Greece and then of Rome. There were democracies in both places—or republics if they were not democracies—which at certain times witnessed the appeal of one man or of one issue, which would come along and sweep away the judgment of the people and play on the passions of the moment. And in the aftermath, what would they find but a ruined and defunct republic and a tyranny in its place.

So they developed these new discoveries, as they saw them—the separation of powers, the independent judiciary, the representation directly and indirectly of people and states in the Congress, a principle that involved not just one majority, but in the most important sense, two majorities.

CONCURRENT MAJORITIES

All through our system we find majorities at work, but they have to be at work simultaneously. John C. Calhoun referred to them as concurrent majorities, and while he often spoke only of the states and the federal government, he perceived a self-evident property of our constitutional arrangements to be found everywhere. The concurrent majority is required between the House of Representatives, based upon the direct election of the people, and a majority in the U.S. Senate. It is a majority of the states that counts in this body, not the majority of the population, *per se*.

Concurrent majorities are also required between sufficient majorities in both houses of Congress and the presidency to enact a law, and the president himself comes to office by having achieved a majority of the electoral votes cast. The power subsequently evolved, but clearly anticipated by the Framers—and I think this is settled—that the Supreme Court could review the acts of Congress and the president in their concurrent majorities, and the majority of the court could judge upon constitutionality. This is a pervasive if not well-understood principle of the Constitution. And of all these majorities, none was more subtle or more central to their thinking than the majorities required to elect a president.

Again there would be two majorities, not in any rigid, absolute sense but in the sense that a clear preponderance of choice would emerge. The president would be elected by a popular vote expressed through the states. That has been our principle ever since. It is the principle enshrined in the Electoral College, and it has been the basic institution that has given structure to American politics, the politics of the presidency.

At an early time in our history, the Electoral College changed its nature from a deliberative body that followed its own will to a body that simply reflected the majority of the electors as they voted in their several states.

While we are a people very much given to the principle of written constitutional arrangements, I believe we have shown a capacity in our government to adopt through practice matters which attain to the condition of principle, as, for example, when early in the republic it became understood that a president would only serve two terms. George Washington established that. And it was a century and a half before it was written into the Constitution. It had the effect of a constitutional principle for all but the experience of one president in a wartime situation, and that was special indeed. That experience led to its being written down as an amendment to the Constitution itself. When, in fact, an informal constitutional principle was violated, it became a formal constitutional provision.

That tradition served us well for a very long period. It served us with respect to the single great problem that republics have always dealt with, which is how to persuade persons in power to leave power. It is a problem that, for example, the republics founded in Latin America in the early nineteenth century have never successfully coped with, or have done so only rarely. This led, in the Mexican Republic, for example, to an eventual recognition that no one ever left power of his own accord, resulting in a constitutional provision for one term and one term only.

In the election of 1800—the most remarkable and most enduring of all political events in our history—the party out of power won an election, and the party in power voluntarily left office. It was John Adams who was defeated when the votes finally came in from the South, and he went back to Quincy, Massachusetts, thinking himself a failure, having turned over the Treasury, the Great Seal, and the Army of the United States to Thomas Jefferson. Far from being a failure, he began democracy in the modern world.

He proved that it could work. It does not work everywhere. We are reduced, to this day, to some 35 democratic societies in the world, about the same number there were in 1914, but the oldest constitutional democracy is ours. And it lives under the Constitution established at the outset, a Constitution established with great sensitivity for the need to see that power is never installed, save when it is consented to by more than one majority. That was the principle of the Electoral College.

MANAGING POLITICAL CONFLICT AND CREATING TRUST

There is another aspect of our Constitution that perhaps is not always recognized, and this aspect concerns the assumption that conflict will exist in political bodies. This is not ordinary; this is unusual.

There is no prior existence anywhere, even in the ancient constitutions of Greece, of this assumption that recognizes that conflict is normal to a political system and needs to be organized and channeled. A much more common assumption was that of monarchy, in which the king is assumed to represent the interests of all, and what the king does is by definition harmonious with the interests of all; or consider the curious doctrine of Karl Marx that such were the basic harmonies of society that, after a period of communism, that the state would wither away, it being coercive by nature and there never being any need to be coercive in a society where natural harmonies had been allowed to evolve.

James Madison knew better. He knew conflict was normal and perpetual. He also believed it could be controlled. And, of course, again, an extra-constitutional institution emerged, one that, interestingly, the Founders had feared, but to which they very clearly lent their formidable energies and enterprise. The *political party* emerged. And from the beginning of our Republic, or to be more precise, from 1796, the third election, political parties developed for the purpose of both organizing conflict *and* limiting conflict.

Only once have we seen them disappear in that brief period, in the 1820s, in the election of 1824, with the first appearance of the so-called faithless elector, when Mr. Plummer of New Hampshire decided that only George Washington should be entitled to the honor of having been unanimously elected by the Electoral College, and so cast his vote for John Quincy Adams. Even there, we see the Electoral College being used as an institution to define majorities, and the parties that emerged had as their single most characteristic quality—again different from anything else in the experience of republics—that they were not ideological, that they were not sectional nor confessional, and never, in the two great parties, extreme.

It is a source of frustration to youth of as many generations as this Republic can measure that our parties have not been extreme. And if we look to the question, why have they not been, the answer is that the Electoral College makes it impossible for them to be if they are to continue effectively to be parties. Indeed, when some have ceased so to do, they have ceased to exist.

The Electoral College requires the assembly of consent—again, concurrent majorities—in one part of the country and another part of the country, and yet another part, all defined in terms of several states. It has as its extraordinary ability the formation of consensus between widely differing regions, political purposes and styles, and political agendas. It has as its purpose and function the narrowing of differences, a narrowing which is repeatedly to be encountered in the narrow range of votes between the parties in presidential elections. Landslides, as we call them!

These landslides are really nothing of the sort. They rarely attain to 60 percent of the vote. When, in fact, one party momentarily belongs to an extreme faction and almost instantly is hugely rebuffed, it has been the experience of two centuries that, just as instantly, they resort to a traditional practice of obtaining consensus, retaining a structure of concurrent majorities around the nation that makes it possible to win a majority of the votes in the Electoral College, and, thereafter, to govern with the legitimacy that has come of attaining to such diverse majorities.

As I have said, the proposal to abolish the Electoral College and replace it with a national plebiscite in the guise of perfecting an alleged weakness in the Constitution, proposes the most radical transformation in our constitutional system that has ever been considered. The Founders devised our system with the idea of a network of concurrent majorities that would be required to exercise power. The fundamental thrust of this measure, however unintended—nonetheless it seems to be ineluctably clear—would be to abolish that principle of concurrent majority.

If there is once introduced into the Constitution the idea that a president may routinely be elected by 40 percent of the vote, you have the most ironic of all outcomes, that in the name of majoritarianism we have abolished even that single majority which the Founders so feared.

OUR FUTURE WITHOUT THE ELECTORAL COLLEGE

Politics is an argument about the future, and no one knows that future. However, as Hamilton and his colleagues argued, the study of history can give you some sense of probabilities. If we would study the modern history of Europe as they studied the ancient history of Greece, would we repeatedly encounter a democratic-republican society succumbing to a plebiscitary majority and to one man and to the end of the republic?

It happened in France; it happened in Italy; it happened in Germany. Almost the only places it has not happened in Europe, on one occasion or another, I dare to suggest, are the constitutional monarchies.

Indeed, there was a moment, not that far distant, when the only democracies left in Europe *were* constitutional monarchies—partly because, having a chief of state, they never had to elect one with real power, and they could govern from their legislatures, where members were elected in individual constituencies, as is the case in Britain today. They never succumbed to the ever-present threat of an overwhelming issue, an over-powering person, and the end of liberty. That is precisely what we invite if we adopt this radical measure.

There are two ways to maintain a political party. Roughly speaking, two models. On the one hand, one can assemble a narrow agenda of issues and find a constituency that cares strongly about those issues and will vote for one's party regardless, as long as it maintains that issue, that purity of doctrine. But that constituency will begin to dissolve when that purity begins to be diluted. That is the fate of democracies where it is not necessary to win a majority of the vote the first time out, and where it becomes possible to take the chance on winning a majority in a runoff.

The nature of the American political party, on the other hand, is that it seeks a majority to begin with. It is broad and has proven to be the despair of every generation of college youth since John Quincy Adams. It tends to mute conflict, to produce little that is inspiring to youth but much that is consoling to age.

What will we see if the Electoral College would be abolished? Well, we do not know what we will see, but we know what others have encountered. We will see a situation in which at the very least we will have four parties because both of the major parties incorporates within itself two parties. One of the great facts of the Electoral College is that after the party convention takes place, the party that loses stays in the party, so to speak. Otherwise, there would be no prospect, even for the minimal rewards that go to the losing faction. There is a disincentive to go out and run on your own.

Conceivably, at least four people would run if the Electoral College was abolished. This would not only become normal, but it would not be abnormal for 14 to run. And you get a kind of randomness in outcome that is characteristic of a purposeless system, and anyone feeling strongly, as people will, and legitimately, about issues, will say: "What if I run and get 19 percent of the vote, and the next highest person gets 24 or 39, and together we go into the runoff, and who knows but that I will emerge?"

This would be a normal and legitimate calculation, a calculation that will have as its most distinguishing characteristic the reality that no longer will anyone take into consideration those units of government—the states—which, as we progress into the twenty-first century, have become indispensable to the management of a governmental system which is increasingly loaded with tasks.

Theodore H. White, in a graphic description of events on election night as he would foresee them, suggests all the drama would leave as the early returns from Massachusetts, South Carolina, and Florida came in and then the great progression across the continent to California, Alaska, and Hawaii. To the contrary, as the undifferentiated votes mounted up, the pressures would be on the mountain states and then the coastal states and the island state, to get out votes, to change outcomes. There would be genuine pressures to fraud and abuse. It would be an election no one understood until the next day or the day after, with recounts that go on forever, and in any event, with no conclusion, and a runoff to come. The drama, the dignity, the decisiveness and finality of the American political system are drained away in an endless sequence of contests, disputed outcomes, and more contests to resolve outcomes already disrupted. That is how legitimacy is lost. That is how a nation trivializes those solemn events that make for the single most important ingredient of a civil society, which is trust.

There was once an acquaintance of mine who served as a diplomatic officer in Southeast Asia during the period of American aid who had a poignant conversation with a friend he had made in that country. As he was leaving, the friend said to him: "You know, you come here and give us this technical assistance and that material assistance, but we know that you never give us the one secret that you have and that we do not, and this secret makes all the difference—which is that you trust one another." And that is what we have to show for two centuries of a Constitution that has made trust possible, partly because it has made conflict visible and manageable.

On March 3, 1858, the *New York Times* reported from Albany that 86 state senators had presented a petition so brief and so explicit that the *Times* gave it in full:

> The undersigned citizens of the State respectfully represent that owing to the great falling off of the canal revenue as well as the increasing drafts upon the State Treasury and the large expenses of carrying on the several departments of the State Government thereby swelling up the taxes, therefore, with the view of relieving the people from the large amount now unnecessarily expended to sustain the executive and legislative departments and to secure the honest and better administration thereof, your petitioners respectfully ask that your honorable body pass an act calling a convention so to alter the Constitution as to abolish both the executive and legislative departments as they now exist and to vest the powers and duties thereof in the President, Vice President, and directors of the New York Central Railroad Company.

The *Times* reported that this was intended as a joke. But in no time at all it passed the Senate. It thereupon passed the assembly, and the following autumn failed of adoption on the ballot by 6,300 votes.

Similarly, some have urged upon us an amendment that would abolish the Democratic and Republican parties and effectively vest their present powers in the president, vice president, and the directors of the National Broadcasting Corporation. The reign of television will be Orwellian and the Republic would decline.

Have we not enough of this? There is a solemn obligation of persons who have been blessed, as we have been blessed, by a stable political system to look to that stability as the most precious inheritance anyone can have. Look about the world and think of the experience of mankind in this generation. Ask what society has lived from 1813 without foreign invasion. Ask what society has never known a break in its congressional or presidential or judicial successions. Ask what society so accepts the principles of the Constitution as to enable the Supreme Court, appointed for life, to strike down laws of this very legislature, and to do so with heightened respect when it fulfills its constitutional mandate. Ask what the legitimacy of justice is once we tinker with the balancing phenomenon of the Electoral College.

We have a republic. It has endured. We trifle with its arrangement at a risk not only to the future of that republic, but, most assuredly, to the reputation of this generation of political men and women.

It is one thing to be, as often we must feel we are, out-thought and out-performed by our predecessors, but are we so to undervalue our own worth as to fall into an almost destructive and adversarial relation to their work?

I respect altogether the purposes that have moved some to propose such an amendment. I suggest they may easily be remedied by an arrangement that abolishes the independence of the elector. Indeed 19 states already require that electors vote as their majority dictates.

There was a time in the nineteenth century when on patriotic occasions, and on almost any occasion that gave the opportunity, Americans would rise and offer the toast to the President and the Constitution of the United States, so intimately did they associate those institutions.

I hope the day does not come when tearing the Constitution asunder we effectively diminish the role of the President of the United States to a man or woman so narrow in his or her base that the opportunity to continue in office, the desire to do so, because of the intensity of factions there that brought the person there in the first place, and the narrowness of base that threatens that incumbency, proceed to animate in the presidency the most un-presidential and anti-republican of temptations.

We have prospered and endured. Let us hope that we shall continue to do so. There is work aplenty before our public councils. Let us get on with that work and leave the Constitution be.

Chapter VII

Creating Constitutional Majorities:
The Electoral College after 2000

Michael M. Uhlmann

The 2000 presidential election was certainly one for the books. Most of them, alas, will probably be written by professors who believe that the will of the people was thwarted, if not by a politically motivated majority of the Supreme Court, then by an outmoded and undemocratic method of presidential election.[1] President Clinton aided their cause in the weeks following the election by questioning both the legitimacy of his successor and the integrity of the High Court. As if on cue, People for the American Way rounded up 585 professors from 112 law schools and took a full-page ad in the *New York Times* that, in so many words, accused five Republican justices of betraying their oath of office.

Despite the temporary lull in public expressions of partisan furor, more along these lines can be expected as Democratic partisans crank their mills in anticipation of the 2002 and 2004 elections. It will be said (a) that Gore was the true choice of the people because he garnered a majority of the national popular vote; and (b) that but for the partisan intervention of the Supreme Court, he would have been

the victor in Florida and thereby the national electoral-vote winner
as well. Although numerous post-election analyses of the Florida vote
confirm that George W. Bush did indeed carry the state, a mythology
of the "stolen" election is almost certain to unfold in the years ahead.
If it does, the constitutional mechanism for electing presidents—which
is badly misunderstood to begin with—will be targeted as an obstacle
to the effectuation of popular will. If the past is prologue, so-called
direct election may once again become a national cause.

I say "so-called," because we already have de facto direct election
of the president, albeit one of a very special kind. It is special because
we conduct that election state-by-state rather than in an undifferentiated national pool, just as we award victory in the World Series to the
winner of four games rather than to the team that scores the most
runs overall. Strictly speaking, of course, voters choose only a slate of
electors pledged to one of the candidates, and it is these electors who
cast the constitutionally binding ballots for president and vice president. As a practical matter, however, the office of elector might as
well not exist. Ever since the 1830s, electors—with but a handful of
exceptions—have faithfully cast their ballots for the popular-vote winner in their states. The "faithless elector" problem (which is easily
enough cured in any event) diverts attention from the larger reform-
ist agenda, which is to establish a national plebiscite in which the
states would be reduced to little more than ministerial agents of a
federal election control authority. The consequences of that step
would alter our political customs and derange our constitutional order as nothing has before. The late Professor Charles Black of Yale
Law School had it right in 1970 when he said that election of the
president by national plebiscite would be "the most deeply radical

amendment that has ever entered the Constitution of the United States."

Why Black and others who share his views reached this conclusion requires reflection of a sort not typically encountered in popular discussions today. The central point to be recognized is that presidential elections are not now, and never have been, a thing apart from the rest of our constitutional and political system. The president is at once the chief executive officer of the Constitution and the most potent political actor in the nation. Our major political parties came into being in the nineteenth century for the primary purpose of capturing the presidency, and that remains their principal goal today. Their structure bears the indelible imprint of the Constitution: The national parties are a loose coalition of state party organizations because the Constitution requires a majority of electoral votes to win. Electoral votes, in turn, are apportioned to the several states in the same manner as seats in Congress.

Presidential elections are thus animated by precisely the same rationale that informs the organization of the national legislature. Dominant weight is given to population, but the weight of numbers is offset by the federal principle, in an effort to constrain the impulse of majority faction, which, as James Madison pointed out, poses the gravest threat to the goals of popular government. This is no mere parchment barrier. By incorporating the federal principle into the mode of presidential election, the Constitution at once connects the presidency to the rest of the constitutional structure, ensures that major political parties will act in concert with that structure, and reminds presidential candidates of the unique character of the nation they seek to lead. Because the states, whether small or large, are the battlegrounds for presidential contests, candidates are forced (often in spite of themselves) to accommodate interests that might otherwise be ignored if popular turnout were the sole criterion for election. Proponents of a "de-federalized" national plebiscite often argue that, as presidents represent "all the people," it must follow that they ought to be elected by the people considered *en masse*. The conclusion disregards the critical consideration: Yes, we are all citizens of a single nation, but that nation is a uniquely federated republic. Although the supremacy of the federal Constitution is acknowledged by all, we take pride as well in the distinct political societies of our home states. The extraordinarily rich diversity of state political cultures acts as a bulwark against centralized administrative authority, and its strength derives in no small part from the constitutional role played by the states in presidential campaigns. Campaigning in New Hampshire is very different from campaigning in California, and representing "all the people" means representing them no less as Texans or New Yorkers than as citizens of an undifferentiated whole.

If the states are removed from the presidential election system, these unique and celebrated features of political locale will lose much of their significance. Voters in the less populous states, indeed in any state that cannot be readily subsumed into a mass media market, will be of decidedly secondary interest to presidential candidates. Politicians naturally gravitate toward the largest pool of voters they can reach at the lowest cost per voter. That necessarily means the larger television markets, where many millions of voters can be reached at a single thrust, regardless of state borders. Mass-market television advertising is expensive, but per capita it is the cheapest route to electoral success when what counts is the sheer number of voters rather than their state of residence. To be sure, mass marketing of this kind already takes place under the current system, but it is constrained by the constitutional necessity of capturing electoral votes. Under a national plebiscite, you can say goodbye forever to state caucuses and primaries, even to national conventions to which delegates now come as members of *state* delegations. What would be their point? And you can bid permanent hello to admen, numbers-crunchers, and spinmeisters, who will care little about what animates voters at the state and local level except insofar as their opinions can be melded into a one-size-fits-all pool of national sentiment. With a national plebiscite, the media mavens will not have to leave their offices in New York, Washington, or Los Angeles to run a presidential campaign. Why should they?

Thanks to the Electoral College, our national political parties are but loose coalitions of state and local units that come together every four years in the effort to win the presidency. With a national plebiscite, this federated structure will disappear, and the ties that bind state and local party affiliates to the national ticket—which are inherently loose to begin with—will be severely weakened. One cannot predict with certainty what will replace these long-standing arrangements, but a good guess is that the current national party committees will be displaced by political operatives paid by or otherwise beholden to rich or powerful candidates, or to sitting presidents. It is also likely that the new power-brokers will be drawn chiefly from the big cities and the near-suburbs, which will become the more or less exclusive theater of presidential campaigns. It cannot be repeated often enough that once the states are severed from presidential campaigns, almost everything you thought you knew about political parties will undergo radical change. As then Senator John F. Kennedy said when defending the Electoral College in the 1950s, changing the mode of presidential elections affects not only presidential candidates but the whole solar system of our constitutional and political arrangements—in ways that are difficult to predict but are likely to be bought at a high price.

All this in the name of trying to ensure...well, what? The fate of the nation would be imperiled, it has been said for years, were a president to be elected with a majority of electoral votes while losing the popular vote. That happened in 2000, but the Capitol still stands and George W. Bush took the oath of office with the applause and good wishes of his fellow citizens ringing in his ears. Despite the ordeal-by-litigation of the Florida imbroglio, and with the exception of a few discontented demagogues who will no doubt be heard from again, the public seems satisfied that the result conformed to constitutional proprieties, and that is enough for them. The last time this sort of thing happened was 1888, with much the same result. (In passing, it should be noted that no one really knows the actual popular vote count in any of the historical examples commonly cited by opponents of the Electoral College.) But an event that occurs once every hundred years or so without imminent peril to the political order is not exactly the stuff of which constitutional crises are made.

The truth is that the electorate in 2000 was so evenly divided that the result was essentially a dead heat. When a hundred million ballots are cast and one has to go to the third decimal place to determine which of two leading candidates won, the public is unlikely to be alarmed no matter who is declared the victor. What seems to matter most to the public in that situation is obedience to the rules and a sense of finality. The final verdict on President Bush's "legitimacy," to the extent it was not conferred by the Constitution itself, will be rendered in November of 2004. To claim that Gore's popular-vote margin of less than one-half of one percent confers some sort of legitimacy that Bush's electoral-vote victory does not is to claim a moral mandate that mere numbers, under the circumstance, lack the power to convey. The claim also ignores the genius of current constitutional arrangements, under which democratic procedure is understood not as an end in itself but as the means to further the goals of democratic government. Those goals have been admirably served by the Electoral College, which has produced a popular-vote majority or plurality for the winner almost every time. And with the relative decline of sectional divisions of the sort that dominated politics in an earlier era, it has also tended to ensure a salutary geographical distribution of the electoral vote for the winner. This simultaneously enhances the winner's ability to govern and constrains political appetites that might veer in constitutionally undesirable directions. (Consider the extraordinary number of states that were closely contested in 2000. Even in victory, President Bush must take care to placate interests in states he carried narrowly.)

The principal reason why the public recognizes Bush's victory as legitimate can be inferred from a quick glance at the 2000 electoral map. His electoral-vote majority was razor-thin, but he carried thirty states and five-sixths of the nation's counties. In a dead-heat election, that provides him with a "democratic" mandate no less plausible than the one claimed by Gore's supporters. The pattern of Gore's state victories was far less dispersed geographically, even though he won the popular vote by a slim margin. It can be argued that his support was far less representative of the nation than was Bush's. It came primarily from areas dominated by big-city machines and mass television markets. Under a national plebiscite of the sort commonly recommended, Gore's geographically skewed pattern, dominated by areas of heavy population density, may be sufficient to carry the country every time. But does such a pattern truly reflect the diversity of American interests? "Direct election" seeks to guarantee popular-vote winners, but only at a price. It cannot guarantee that the popular vote will adequately mirror the nation, and for that reason cannot guarantee that a popular-vote winner will be able to govern fairly or effectively.

The Framers, in their wisdom, understood the limits of simple-minded majoritarianism of the sort embraced by proposals for a geographically undifferentiated national plebiscite. If elections were simply a matter of counting heads and stopping when you got to 50 percent plus one, we could dispense with all the checks and balances of the Constitution, including federalism, bicameralism, the separation of powers, staggered elections, even the United States Senate itself. The point of these time-honored devices, including the Electoral College, is not to circumvent popular sentiment, but to shape and channel it in a fashion that supports the ends for which popular government is constituted. Majority rule can become majority tyranny, as the wisest students of politics have always known. The trick in establishing popular government is to empower the majority without endangering the rights of minorities. That is precisely what the Constitution's checks and balances, in whole and in part, seek to do. Thomas Jefferson said it well in his First Inaugural Address, following one of the most bitterly contested elections in American history:

"All, too, will bear in mind this sacred principle, that though the will of the majority is in all cases to prevail, that will to be rightful must be reasonable; that the minority possess their equal rights, which equal law must protect, and to violate which would be oppression."

In short, not just any majority will do in a government dedicated to protecting the equal rights of all. One must pay heed not only to the numerical size of a winning coalition, but to the manner of its composition. The Electoral College is not perfect—no election system can be—but it has been notably successful in election after election in producing Jefferson's reasonable majorities. That is no small accomplishment in a nation of this size and diversity. Political passions run deep precisely because they express our sense of what is just, not only for ourselves but for the country. When our favored candidate loses, we are of course disappointed, sometimes heatedly so, that our policy preferences will not so easily be advanced. But we do not generally have to worry that the winning party will endanger our basic rights. Part of the reason is that the electoral-vote system, reinforced by the winner-take-all custom that prevails in 48 states, requires serious national candidates to solicit support from most of the same voters. Gore's great strength lay in large urban areas, but he could not safely disregard voters or interests in other regions. Whatever candidates might wish if they had their druthers, the electoral-vote system drives them toward the center, for the same reason that presidents also take care to govern from the center. Winner-take-all also induces interest groups, in turn, to moderate their demands and to accommodate them as best they can to both major parties.

Under direct election, these incentives toward moderation on the part of candidates and interest groups would be severely weakened. A national plebiscite conducted without reference to winner-take-all in the states (indeed, without reference to the states at all) has no mechanism to ensure that both major party candidates will appeal to all or most of the same voters; it has no mechanism to ensure that they will carry their campaigns across the breadth of the land, and none to encourage factions to moderate their demands; it has no effective way of ensuring that, most of the time, there will be two and only two major candidates. It has no mechanism, in short, to ensure that the majority coalition will be reasonable, in Jefferson's sense, either during the campaign or after it acquires power. The United States has never known plebiscitary politics of the sort envisioned by direct election. While one cannot say for sure, the likely result will be much sharper ideological and geographical divisions. And because direct election will almost certainly produce a runoff election every time, there will be little incentive for candidates to moderate their stands until after the first vote. Political moderation does not occur by accident, nor because politicians are inherently nicer people than the rest of us. Election systems are not the only means of inducing compromise, but they exert powerful influence over the strategy, conduct, and rhetoric of campaigns; they channel political ambition in socially constructive or destructive ways.

We cannot say for sure what form political ambition will take under a national plebiscite. But we know this much: that it would be most unwise, even dangerous, to disconnect our chief executive from the Electoral College without compensating for the loss of its moderating influences. Take another look at the electoral map of 2000 and ask yourself what incentives to compromise would exist the next time around under direct election. Take another look and ask how much voters in less populous states would matter in a mass-market media campaign. Take another look at the Florida squabble and ask whether we would be better of if similar squabbles took place simultaneously in a dozen places throughout the country, as they almost certainly would under a national plebiscite. And ask yourself which system is more likely to discourage and contain fraud. (There are approximately 180,000 polling places in the United States. Under direction election, as Everett Dirksen might say, a few votes here, and a few votes there, and pretty soon it all adds up.)

Ever since the presidency became a popularly elective office, campaigns have been conducted state-by-state. Most of our political customs, expectations, and opinions about presidential politics are informed and mediated by the principles of federalism. Indeed, those principles are so deeply embedded in our political thinking that we scarcely reflect on their importance. What holds true for citizens generally has an even deeper influence on presidential candidates, who learn much about this nation's incredible diversity by being forced to campaign throughout the country. They also learn, in ways that textbooks cannot adequately convey, about America's unique constitutional structure and the unique political culture it inspires. Once election to the presidency is severed from the rest of our constitutional structure, new incentives will be created, and new lessons taught, none of which will have much to do with the way elections have been conducted in the past. If "the will of the people" is understood to convey legitimacy separate and apart from the constitutional system and the goals it was designed to ensure, how shall we constrain a president who claims the "moral mandate" of popular will as his reason for ignoring constitutional strictures once in office?

Afterword

Outputs: The Electoral College Produces Presidents

WALTER BERNS

On January 8, 1981, following the election in which John
Anderson ran as an independent candidate, I began a *Wall
Street Journal* article under the title "Let's Hear It for the Electoral
College," by pointing out that "where the Electoral College is concerned, nothing fails to succeed like success." By success I meant it
regularly produces a president with a clear and immediate claim to the
office, in part because it exaggerates the margin of victory in the
popular vote. It did this in 1980 and, until 2000, in every subsequent
election, but this did not satisfy its critics, some of whom have made
a career of proposing constitutional amendments to abolish it.

Their complaints are familiar. The Electoral College, we are told,
is a "relic," an "absurdly dangerous" method of selecting a president
that threatens to "plunge the nation into political chaos." The pre-
sumed danger is that a candidate might receive a majority of the electoral votes while receiving fewer popular votes than his or her opponent. The critics speak of the popular vs. electoral vote discrepancy as
a "time bomb waiting to go off," but the last time it did go off, in

1888, nothing happened. There was hardly a ripple of popular discontent, no spate of editorials claiming that Benjamin Harrison was an illegitimate president, no complaints from the losing candidate, Grover Cleveland, that he had been cheated. Indeed, when asked by a reporter the day after the election to what he attributed his defeat, Cleveland smiled and said, "It was mainly because the other party got more votes."

It was different this past year. No sooner had the election results been reported than Al Gore's campaign chairman claimed fraud, and Hillary Rodham Clinton (and even Senator Arlen Specter) said that the Electoral College had to be abolished in favor of a direct popular vote. Editorialists, newspaper journalists, and television pundits subsequently joined the chorus.

Have we really reached the point where the right to hold an office depends *solely* on the suffrage of a popular majority? Are the sponsors of the proposed constitutional amendments willing to say that a candidate elected with a *constitutional* but not a popular majority is an illegitimate president? Perhaps, but only if the moral authority of the Electoral College—indeed, of the Constitution itself—has been undermined by the persistent efforts to get rid of it, especially the efforts of members of Congress and what the British call the "chattering class."

The Electoral College is said to be undemocratic, a violation of the democratic principles of "one-man, one-vote" and majority rule. In fact, however, the majority now rules, but at the state level, where (except in Maine and Nebraska) the votes are aggregated. As it happens, this is where the vote of any particular minority looms larger, or carries more weight, than it is likely to do in the country as a whole. So long as a minority is not distributed evenly throughout the country, it is in its interest to oppose direct popular elections; civil rights leaders used to understand this. And is there not something to be said for an electoral system that threatens to penalize a political party and its candidate for failing to respect the rights of respectable minorities? Furthermore, is there not something to be said for an electoral system that protects the interests of states as states, which is to say, a system with an element of federalism built into it? Only twice in this century (1960 and 1976) has the candidate with an Electoral College majority failed to win a majority of the states. And is there not, then, something to be said for a system that threatens to penalize sectional candidates who cannot attract a more general national constituency?

The American idea of democracy cannot be expressed in the simple but insidious formula, "the greatest good for the greatest number." What the greatest number regards as its greatest good might very well prove to be a curse to those who are not part of that number. The American idea of democracy, which is expressed in the Declaration of Independence and embodied in various provisions of the Constitution, is that government is instituted to secure the rights of all. What is constitutionalism if it is not a qualification of majoritarianism?

The men who founded this country surely recognized the entitlements of a popular majority, but, with an eye to the qualifications or qualities required of an office, they devised institutions—the Electoral College is one of them—that modify or qualify the majoritarian principle. Nothing could be clearer than that the Founders sought institutions or ways—Tocqueville called them "forms"—that would protect the country from what has come to be called populism. The organizing principle of the Senate is surely not majority rule, nor are its procedures purely democratic. Federal judges are not elected at all. If legitimacy springs only from the principle of "one man, one (equally weighted) vote," upon what meat do these judicial Caesars feed? If populism is our only principle, why stop with the people's vote? Why not select all public officials by lot? This would be truly democratic, because it pays no attention whatsoever to the qualifications of office holders—or else assumes that everyone is equally qualified. In short, the issue that ought to engage our attention is the one the Framers debated over the entire course of the constitutional convention, namely, "What system is more likely to produce a president with the qualities required of the person who holds this great office?" In all the years I have been engaged with this issue, I have yet to encounter a critic of the Electoral College who argues that a president chosen directly by the people is likely to be a *better* president.

My argument was best made by the late Professor Herbert Storing when, in 1977, he testified before the sub-committee on the Constitution of the Senate Judiciary Committee. He said,

> To see the case for the present system of electing the president requires a shift in point of view from that usually taken by the critics [of the Electoral College]. They tend to view elections in terms of *input*—in terms of the right to vote, equal weight of votes, who in fact votes, and the like. The framers [of the Constitution] thought it at least as important to consider the *output* of any given electoral system. What kind of men does it bring to office? How will it affect the working of the political system? What is its bearing on the political character of the whole country?

If James Madison, Alexander Hamilton, James Wilson, Benjamin Franklin, Gouverneur Morris, and the rest thought it important to consider *output* as well as *input* when designing the electoral system, I think that we today are obliged to do the same when considering proposals to amend it. This remains a question that perennial enemies of the Electoral College never seem willing to entertain.

Appendix I

Article II and the Twelfth Amendment to the Constitution

Reprinted here is Article II of the Constitution, where the mechanism for electing the president of the United States is found. Though George Washington was able to hold the nation together without a formal party system, almost immediately upon his passing from the political scene the rival factions of Federalists (led by John Adams and Alexander Hamilton) and Republicans (led by Thomas Jefferson and James Madison) coalesced as opposing camps.

This nascent party system led to the crisis election of 1800. Because electors at that time cast two votes on one slip of paper, the two Republican candidates for president and vice president ended up in a tie—there was no way to differentiate one's vote between the presidential and vice presidential candidates. The House of Representatives, which was still under the control of the Federalist party, then had to choose among the Republican candidates for president and vice president. In 1804 the Constitution was amended to iron out the flaws in the electoral system that this election laid bare. The result was the Twelfth Amendment to the Constitution, which is reprinted here following Article II.

Article II

Section 1

1. The executive Power shall be vested in a President of the United States of America. He shall hold his Office during the Term of four Years, and, together with the Vice President, chosen for the same term, be elected, as follows:

2. Each State shall appoint, in such Manner as the Legislature thereof may direct, a Number of Electors, equal to the whole number of Senators and Representatives to which the State may be entitled in the Congress: but no Senator or Representative, or Person holding an Office of Trust or Profit under the United States, shall be appointed an Elector.

3. [The Electors shall meet in their respective States, and vote by Ballot for two Persons, of whom one at least shall not be an Inhabitant of the same State with themselves. And they shall make a List of all the Persons voted for, and of the Number of Votes for each; which List they shall sign and certify, and transmit sealed to the Seat of the Government of the United States, directed to the President of the Senate. The President of the Senate shall, in the Presence of the Senate and House of Representatives, open all the Certificates, and the Votes shall then be counted. The Person having the greatest Number of Votes shall be the President, if such Number be a Majority of the whole Number of Electors appointed; and if there be more than one who have such Majority and have an equal Number of Votes,

then the House of Representatives shall immediately choose by Ballot one of them for President; and if no Person have a Majority, then from the five highest on the list the said House shall in like Manner choose the President. But in choosing the President, the Votes shall be taken by States, the Representation from each State having one Vote; A quorum for this Purpose shall consist of a Member or Members from two thirds of the States, and a Majority of all the States shall be necessary to a Choice. In every Case, after the Choice of the President, the Person having the greatest Number of Votes of the electors shall be the Vice President. But if there should remain two or more who have equal Votes, the Senate shall choose from them by Ballot the Vice President.][1]

4. The Congress may determine the Time of choosing the Electors, and the Day on which they shall give their Votes; which Day shall be the same throughout the United States.

5. No Person, except a natural-born Citizen, or a Citizen of the United States at the time of the Adoption of this Constitution, shall be eligible to that Office of President; neither shall any Person be eligible to that Office who shall not have attained to the Age of thirty-five Years, and been fourteen years a Resident within the United States.

6. In Case of the Removal of the President from Office, or of his Death, Resignation, or Inability to discharge the Powers and Duties of the said Office, the Same shall devolve on the Vice President, and the Congress may by Law provide for the Case of Removal, Death, Resignation, or Inability, both the President and Vice President, declaring what Officer shall then act as President, and such Officer shall act accordingly, until the Disability be removed, or a President shall be elected.

7. The President shall, at stated Times, receive for his Services, a Compensation, which shall neither be increased nor diminished during the Period for which he shall have been elected, and he shall not receive within that Period any other Emolument from the United States, or any of them.

8. Before he enter on the Execution of his Office, he shall take the following Oath or affirmation:—"I do solemnly swear (or affirm) that I will faithfully execute the Office of the President of the United States, and will, to the best of my Ability, preserve, protect, and defend the Constitution of the United States."

Section 2

1. The President shall be Commander in Chief of the Army and Navy of the United States, and of the Militia of the several States, when called into the actual Service of the United States; he may require the Opinion, in writing, of the principal Officer in each of the executive Departments, upon any Subject relating to the Duties of their respective Offices, and he shall have the Power to grant Reprieves and Pardons for Offences against the United States, except in Cases of Impeachment.

2. He shall have Power, by and with the Advice and Consent of the Senate, to make Treaties, provided two thirds of the Senators present concur; and he shall nominate, and by and with the Advice and Consent of the Senate, shall appoint, Ambassadors, other public Ministers, and Consuls, Judges of the supreme Court, and all other Officers of the United States, whose Appointments are not herein otherwise provided for, and which shall be established by Law; but the Congress may by Law vest the Appointment of such inferior Of-

ficers, as they think proper, in the President alone, in the Courts of Law, or in the Heads of Departments.

3. The President shall have Power to fill up all Vacancies that may happen during the Recess of the Senate, by granting Commissions which shall expire at the End of their next Session.

Section 3

He shall from time to time give to the Congress Information of the State of the Union, and recommend to their Consideration such Measures as he shall judge necessary and expedient; he may, on extraordinary Occasions, convene both Houses, or either of them, and in Case of Disagreement between them, with Respect to the Time of Adjournment, he may adjourn them to such Time as he shall think proper; he shall receive Ambassadors and other public Ministers; he shall take Care that the Laws be faithfully executed, and shall Commission all the Officers of the United States.

Section 4

The President, Vice President and all civil Officers of the United States, shall be removed from Office on Impeachment for, and Conviction of, Treason, Bribery, or other high Crimes and Misdemeanors.

AMENDMENT XII
(Ratified June 15, 1804)

The Electors shall meet in their respective states and vote by ballot for President and Vice-President, one of whom, at least, shall not be an inhabitant of the same state with themselves; they shall name in their ballots the person voted for as President, and in distinct ballots the person voted for as Vice-President, and of the number of votes for each, which lists they shall sign and certify, and transmit sealed to the seat of the government of the United States, directed to the President of the Senate—The President of the Senate shall, in the presence of the Senate and House of Representatives, open all the certificates and the votes shall then be counted;—The person having the greatest number of votes for President, shall be the President, if such number be a majority of the whole number of Electors appointed; and if no person have such majority, then from the persons having the highest numbers not exceeding three on the list of those voted for as President, the House of Representatives shall choose immediately, by ballot, the President. But in choosing the President, the votes shall be taken by states, the representation from each state having one vote; a quorum for this purpose shall consist of a member or members from two-thirds of the states, and a majority of all the states shall be necessary to a choice. [And if the House of Representatives shall not choose a President whenever the right of choice shall devolve upon them, before the fourth day of March next following, then the Vice-

President shall act as President, as in the case of the death or other constitutional disability of the President—]² The person having the greatest number of votes as Vice-President, shall be the Vice-President, if such number be a majority of the whole number of Electors appointed, and if no person have a majority, then from the two highest numbers on the list, the Senate shall choose the Vice-President; a quorum for the purpose shall consist of two-thirds of the whole number of Senators, and a majority of the whole number shall be necessary to a choice. But no person constitutionally ineligible to the office of President shall be eligible to that of Vice-President of the United States.

Appendix II

Federalist Papers *39 and 68*

The Federalist Papers *were originally a series of newspaper editorials written by James Madison, Alexander Hamilton, and John Jay during the fall and winter of 1787–1788 to support the ratification of the new Constitution. They are widely recognized as the single most important statement of the founding generation on the original meaning of the Constitution, and they may be the most important contribution of American civilization to the history of political ideas. Thomas Jefferson, for instance, almost immediately recognized their significance, calling them in 1788 "the best commentary on the principles of government, which ever was written."*

Reprinted in this appendix are papers 39 and 68. In Federalist 39, James Madison outlines the new constitutional system, finding it to be complex and balanced, allowing important roles to be played by the states, and always adhering to republican principles. The constitutional method of presidential selection is one important part of that complex and balanced system. In Federalist 68, Alexander Hamilton lays out the original understanding of the Electoral College as an institution that would afford the nation a "moral certainty" that the office of president of the United States would always be filled with men having "the requisite qualifications" for high office.

Federalists 39 and 68 are reprinted here from an 1818 edition published in Washington, D.C., by Jacob Gideon Jr.

No. 39

BY JAMES MADISON

The conformity of the plan to republican principles: an objection in respect to the powers of the convention, examined.

The last paper having concluded the observations, which were meant to introduce a candid survey of the plan of government reported by the convention, we now proceed to the execution of that part of our undertaking.

The first question that offers itself is, whether the general form and aspect of the government be strictly republican? It is evident that no other form would be reconcileable with the genius of the people of America; with the fundamental principles of the revolution; or with that honourable determination which animates every votary of freedom, to rest all our political experiments on the capacity of mankind for self-government. If the plan of the convention, therefore, be found to depart from the republican character, its advocates must abandon it as no longer defensible.

What then are the distinctive characters of the republican form? Were an answer to this question to be sought, not by recurring to principles, but in the application of the term by political writers, to the constitutions of different states, no satisfactory one would ever be found. Holland, in which no particle of the supreme authority is derived from the people, has passed almost universally under the denomination of a republic. The same title has been bestowed on Venice, where absolute power over the great body of the people is exercised, in the most absolute manner, by a small body of hereditary nobles. Poland, which is a mixture of aristocracy and of monarchy in their worst forms, has been dignified with the same appellation. The government of England, which has one republican branch only, combined with a hereditary aristocracy and monarchy, has, with equal impropriety, been frequently placed on the list of republics. These examples, which are nearly as dissimilar to each other as to a genuine republic, show the extreme inaccuracy with which the term has been used in political disquisitions.

If we resort for a criterion, to the different principles on which different forms of government are established, we may define a republic to be, or at least may bestow that name on, a government which derives all its powers directly or indirectly from the great body of the people; and is administered by persons holding their offices during pleasure, for a limited period, or during good behaviour. It is *essential* to such a government, that it be derived from the great body of the society, not from an inconsiderable proportion, or a favoured class of it; otherwise a handful of tyrannical nobles, exercising their oppressions by a delegation of their powers, might aspire to the rank of republicans, and claim for their government the honourable title of republic. It is *sufficient* for such a government, that the persons administering it be appointed, either directly or indirectly, by the people; and that they hold their appointments by either of the tenures just specified; otherwise every government in the United States, as well as every other popular government that has been, or can be well organized or well executed, would be degraded from the republican character. According to the constitution of every state in the union, some or other of the officers of government are appointed indirectly only by the people. According to most of them, the chief magistrate himself is so appointed. And according to one, this mode of appointment is extended to one of the co-ordinate branches of the legislature. According to all the constitutions also, the tenure of the highest offices is extended to a definite period, and in many instances, both within the legislative and executive departments, to a period of years. According to the provisions of most of the constitutions, again, as well as according to the most respectable and received opinions on the subject, the members of the judiciary department are to retain their offices by the firm tenure of good behaviour.

On comparing the constitution planned by the convention, with the standard here fixed, we perceive at once, that it is, in the most rigid sense, conformable to it. The house of representatives, like that of one branch at least of all the state legislatures, is elected immediately by the great body of the people. The senate, like the present congress, and the senate of Maryland, derives its appointment indirectly from the people. The president is indirectly derived from the choice of the people, according to the example in most of the states. Even the judges, with all other officers of the union, will, as in the several states, be the choice, though a remote choice, of the people themselves. The duration of the appointments is equally conformable to the republican standard, and to the model of the state constitutions. The house of representatives is periodically elective, as in all the states; and for the period of two years, as in the state of South

Carolina. The senate is elective, for the period of six years; which is but one year more than the period of the senate of Maryland; and but two more than that of the senates of New York and Virginia. The president is to continue in office for the period of four years; as in New York and Delaware, the chief magistrate is elected for three years, and in South Carolina for two years. In the other states the election is annual. In several of the states, however, no explicit provision is made for the impeachment of the chief magistrate. And in Delaware and Virginia, he is not impeachable till out of office. The president of the United States is impeachable at any time during his continuance in office. The tenure by which the judges are to hold their places, is, as it unquestionably ought to be, that of good behaviour. The tenure of the ministerial offices generally, will be a subject of legal regulation, conformably to the reason of the case, and the example of the state constitutions.

Could any further proof be required of the republican complexion of this system, the most decisive one might be found in its absolute prohibition of titles of nobility, both under the federal and the state governments; and in its express guarantee of the republican form to each of the latter.

But it was not sufficient, say the adversaries of the proposed constitution, for the convention to adhere to the republican form. They ought, with equal care, to have preserved the *federal* form, which regards the union as a *confederacy* of sovereign states; instead of which, they have framed a *national* government, which regards the union as a *consolidation* of the states. And it is asked, by what authority this bold and radical innovation was undertaken? The handle which has been made of this objection requires, that it should be examined with some precision.

Without inquiring into the accuracy of the distinction on which the objection is founded, it will be necessary to a just estimate of its force, first, to ascertain the real character of the government in question; secondly, to inquire how far the convention were authorized to propose such a government; and thirdly, how far the duty they owed to their country, could supply any defect of regular authority.

First. In order to ascertain the real character of the government, it may be considered in relation to the foundation on which it is to be established; to the sources from which its ordinary powers are to be drawn; to the operation of those powers; to the extent of them; and to the authority by which future changes in the government are to be introduced.

On examining the first relation, it appears, on one hand, that the constitution is to be founded on the assent and ratification of the people of America, given by deputies elected for the special purpose; but on the other, that this assent and ratification is to be given by the people, not as individuals composing one entire nation, but as composing the distinct and independent states to which they respectively belong. It is to be the assent and ratification of the several states, derived from the supreme authority in each state....the authority of the people themselves. The act, therefore, establishing the constitution, will not be a *national*, but a *federal* act.

That it will be a federal, and not a national act, as these terms are understood by the objectors, the act of the people, as forming so many independent states, not as forming one aggregate nation, is obvious from this single consideration, that it is to result neither from the decision of a *majority* of the people of the union, nor from that of a *majority* of the states. It must result from the *unanimous* assent of the several states that are parties to it, differing no otherwise from their ordinary assent than in its being expressed, not by the legislative authority, but by that of the people themselves. Were the people regarded in this transaction as forming one nation, the will of the majority of the whole people of the United States would bind the minority; in the same manner as the majority in each state must bind the minority; and the will of the majority must be determined either by a comparison of the individual votes, or by considering the will of the majority of the states, as evidence of the will of a majority of the people of the United States. Neither of these rules has been adopted. Each state, in ratifying the constitution, is considered as a sovereign body, independent of all others, and only to be bound by its own voluntary act. In this relation, then, the new constitution will, if established, be a *federal*, and not a *national* constitution.

The next relation is, to the sources from which the ordinary powers of government are to be derived. The house of representatives will derive its powers from the people of America, and the people will be represented in the same proportion, and on the same principle, as they are in the legislature of a particular state. So far the government is *national*, not *federal*. The senate, on the other hand, will derive its powers from the states, as political and co-equal societies; and these will be represented on the principle of equality in the senate, as they now are in the existing congress. So far the government is *federal*, not *national*. The executive power will be derived from a very compound source. The immediate election of the president is to be made by the states in their political characters. The votes alloted to them are in a compound ratio, which considers them partly as distinct and co-equal societies; partly as unequal members of the same society. The eventual election, again, is to be made by that branch of the legislature which consists of the national representatives; but in this particular act, they are to be thrown into the form of individual delegations, from so many distinct and co-equal bodies politic. From this aspect of the government, it appears to be of a mixed character, presenting at least as many *federal* as *national* features.

The difference between a federal and national government, as it relates to the *operation of the government,* is, by the adversaries of the plan of the convention, supposed to consist in this, that in the former, the powers operate on the political bodies composing the confederacy, in their political capacities; in the latter, on the individual citizens composing the nation, in their individual capacities. On trying the constitution by this criterion, it falls under the *national,* not the *federal* character; though perhaps not so completely as has been understood. In several cases, and particularly in the trial of controversies to which states may be parties, they must be viewed and proceeded against in their collective and political capacities only. But the operation of the government on the people in their individual capacities, in its ordinary and most essential proceedings, will, on the whole, in the sense of its opponents, designate it in this relation, a *national* government.

But if the government be national, with regard to the *operation* of its powers, it changes its aspect again, when we contemplate it in relation to the *extent* of its powers. The idea of a national government involves in it, not only an authority over the individual citizens, but an indefinite supremacy over all persons and things, so far as they are objects of lawful government. Among a people consolidated into one nation, this supremacy is completely vested in the national legislature. Among communities united for particular purposes, it is vested partly in the general, and partly in the municipal legislatures. In the former case, all local authorities are subordinate to the supreme; and may be controled, directed, or abolished by it at pleasure. In the latter, the local or municipal authorities form distinct and independent portions of the supremacy, no more subject, within their respective spheres; to the general authority, than the general authority is subject to them within its own sphere. In this relation, then, the proposed government cannot be deemed a *national* one; since its jurisdiction extends to certain enumerated objects only, and leaves to the several states, a residuary and inviolable sovereignty over all other objects. It is true, that in controversies relating to the boundary between the two jurisdictions, the tribunal which is ultimately to decide, is to be established under the general government. But this does not change the principle of the case. The decision is to be impartially made, according to the rules of the constitution; and all the usual and most effectual precautions are taken to secure this impartiality. Some such tribunal is clearly essential to prevent an appeal to the sword, and a dissolution of the compact; and that it ought to be established under the general, rather than under the local governments; or, to speak more properly, that it could be safely established under the first alone, is a position not likely to be combated.

If we try the constitution by its last relation, to the authority by which amendments are to be made, we find it neither wholly *national*, nor wholly *federal*. Were it wholly national, the supreme and ultimate authority would reside in the *majority* of the people of the union; and this authority would be competent at all times, like that of a majority of every national society, to alter or abolish its established government. Were it wholly federal on the other hand, the concurrence of each state in the union would be essential to every alteration that would be binding on all. The mode provided by the plan of the convention, is not founded on either of these principles. In requiring more than a majority, and particularly, in computing the proportion by *states*, not by *citizens*, it departs from the *national*, and advances towards the *federal* character. In rendering the concurrence of less than the whole number of states sufficient, it loses again the *federal*, and partakes of the *national* character.

The proposed constitution, therefore, even when tested by the rules laid down by its antagonists, is, in strictness, neither a national nor a federal constitution; but a composition of both. In its foundation it is federal, not national; in the sources from which the ordinary powers of the government are drawn, it is partly federal, and partly national; in the operation of these powers, it is national, not federal; in the extent of them again, it is federal, not national; and finally, in the authoritative mode of introducing amendments, it is neither wholly federal, nor wholly national.

PUBLIUS

No. 68

BY ALEXANDER HAMILTON

The view of the constitution of the president continued, in relation to the mode of appointment.

The mode of appointment of the chief magistrate of the United States, is almost the only part of the system, of any consequence, which has escaped without severe censure, or which has received the slightest mark of approbation from its opponents. The most plausible of these, who has appeared in print, has even deigned to admit, that the election of the president is pretty well guarded.* I venture somewhat further, and hesitate not to affirm, that if the manner of it be not perfect, it is at least excellent. It unites in an eminent degree all the advantages, the union of which was to be wished for.

It was desirable, that the sense of the people should operate in the choice of the person to whom so important a trust was to be confided. This end will be answered by committing the right of making it, not to any pre-established body, but to men chosen by the people for the special purpose, and at the particular conjuncture.

It was equally desirable, that the immediate election should be made by men most capable of analyzing the qualities adapted to the station, and acting under circumstances favourable to deliberation, and to a judicious combination of all the reasons and inducements that were proper to govern their choice. A small number of persons, selected by their fellow citizens from the general mass, will be most likely to possess the information and discernment requisite to so complicated an investigation.

It was also peculiarly desirable, to afford as little opportunity as possible to tumult and disorder. This evil was not least to be dreaded in the election of a magistrate, who was to have so important an agency in the administration of the government. But the precautions which have been so happily concerted in the system under consideration, promise an effectual security against this mischief. The choice of *several*, to form an intermediate body of electors, will be much less apt to convulse the community, with any extraordinary or violent movements, than the choice of *one*, who was himself to be the final object of the public wishes. And as the electors, chosen in each state, are to assemble and vote in the state in which they are chosen, this detached and divided situation will expose them much less to heats and ferments, that might be communicated from them to the people, than if they were all to be convened at one time, in one place.

Nothing was more to be desired, than that every practicable obstacle should be opposed to cabal, intrigue, and corruption. These most deadly adversaries of republican government, might naturally have been expected to make their approaches from more than one quarter, but chiefly from the desire in foreign powers to gain an improper ascendant in our councils. How could they better gratify this, than by raising a creature of their own to the chief magistracy of the union? But the convention have guarded against all danger of this sort, with the most provident and judicious attention. They have not made the appointment of the president to depend on pre-existing bodies of men, who might be tampered with beforehand to prostitute their votes; but they have referred it in the first instance to an immediate act of the people of America, to be exerted in the choice of persons for the temporary and sole purpose of making the appointment. And they have excluded from eligibility to this trust, all those who from situation might be suspected of too great devotion to the president in office. No senator, representative, or other person holding a place of trust or profit under the United States, can be of the number of the electors. Thus, without corrupting the body of the people, the immediate agents in the election will at least enter upon the task, free from any sinister bias. Their transient existence, and their detached situation, already noticed, afford a satisfactory prospect of their continuing so, to the conclusion of it. The business of corruption, when it is to embrace so considerable a number of men, requires time, as well as means. Nor would it be found easy suddenly to embark them, dispersed as they would be over thirteen states, in any combinations founded upon motives which, though they could not properly be denominated corrupt, might yet be of a nature to mislead them from their duty.

Another, and no less important, desideratum was, that the executive should be independent for his continuance in office, on all but the people themselves. He might otherwise be tempted to sacrifice his duty to his complaisance for those whose favour was necessary to the duration of his official consequence. This advantage will also be secured, by making his re-election to depend on a special body of representatives, deputed by the society for the single purpose of making the important choice.

All these advantages will be happily combined in the plan devised by the convention, which is, that each state shall choose a number of persons as electors, equal to the number of senators and repre-

sentatives of such state in the national government, who shall assemble within the state, and vote for some fit person as president.
Their votes, thus given, are to be transmitted to the seat of the national government; and the person who may happen to have a majority of the whole number of votes, will be the president. But as a majority of the votes might not always happen to centre in one man,
and as it might be unsafe to permit less than a majority to be conclu-
sive, it is provided, that, in such a contingency, the house of representatives shall select out of the candidates, who shall have the five
highest numbers of votes, the man who, in their opinion, may be
best qualified for the office.

This process of election affords a moral certainty, that the office
of president will seldom fail to the lot of any man who is not in an
eminent degree endowed with the requisite qualifications. Talents
for low intrigue, and the little arts of popularity, may alone suffice to
elevate a man to the first honours of a single state; but it will require
other talents, and a different kind of merit, to establish him in the
esteem and confidence of the whole union, or of so considerable a
portion of it, as would be necessary to make him a successful candidate for the distinguished office of president of the United States. It
will not be too strong to say, that there will be a constant probability
of seeing the station filled by characters pre-eminent for ability and
virtue. And this will be thought no inconsiderable recommendation
of the constitution, by those who are able to estimate the share which
the executive in every government must necessarily have in its good
or ill administration. Though we cannot acquiesce in the political
heresy of the poet, who says

"For forms of government, let fools contest....
"That which is best administered, is best;"

yet we may safely pronounce, that the true test of a good government is, its aptitude and tendency to produce a good administration.

The vice-president is to be chosen in the same manner with the president; with this difference, that the senate is to do, in respect to the former, what is to be done by the house of representatives, in respect to the latter.

The appointment of an extraordinary person, as vice-president, has been objected to as superfluous, if not mischievous. It has been alleged, that it would have been preferable to have authorized the senate to elect out of their own body an officer answering to that description. But two considerations seem to justify the ideas of the convention in this respect. One is, that to secure at all times the possibility of a definite resolution of the body, it is necessary that the president should have only a casting vote. And to take the senator of any state from his seat as senator, to place him in that of president of the senate, would be to exchange, in regard to the state from which he came, a constant for a contingent vote. The other consideration is, that, as the vice-president may occasionally become a substitute for the president, in the supreme executive magistracy, all the reasons which recommend the mode of election prescribed for the one, apply with great, if not with equal force to the manner of appointing the other. It is remarkable, that, in this, as in most other instances, the objection which is made, would lie against the constitution of this state. We have a lieutenant-governor, chosen by the people at large, who presides in the senate, and is the constitutional substitute for the governor in casualties similar to those which would authorize the vice-president to exercise the authorities, and discharge the duties of the president.

PUBLIUS

* Vide Federal Farmer.

Notes

Chapter I
The Origins and Meaning of the Electoral College
GARY L. GREGG II

1. For examples of such an interpretation of the Electoral College, see James MacGregor Burns, *The Power to Lead: The Crisis in the American Presidency* (New York: Simon and Schuster, 1984); Richard M. Pious, *The American Presidency* (New York: Basic Books, 1979); Craig A. Rimmerman, *Presidency by Plebiscite: The Reagan-Bush Era in Institutional Perspective* (Boulder, Colo.: Westview Press, 1993); Robert E. DiClerico, *The American President*, Fourth Edition (Englewood Cliffs, N.J.: Prentice Hall, 1995).

2. Max Farrand, ed. *The Records of the Federal Convention of 1787* (New Haven, Conn.: Yale University Press, 1966), vol. 1, 68. All subsequent references to the Constitutional Convention in this chapter are from this edition.

3. Farrand, *Records of the Federal Convention of 1787*, vol. 1, 69.

4. Ibid., 29.

5. George Mason, for instance, "conceived it would be as unnatural to refer the choice of a proper character for chief Magistrate to the people, as it would, to refer a trial of colours to a blind man" (Farrand, vol. 2, 31).

6. Farrand, *Records of the Federal Convention of 1787*, vol. 1, 68.

7. Farrand, *Records of the Federal Convention of 1787*, vol. 2, 56.

8. Ibid., 33.

9. Ibid., 56.

10. Ibid., 56.

11. Ibid., 101, 109.

12. Ibid., 500.

13. Isaac Kramnick, ed. *The Federalist Papers*, 39 (England: Penguin Books, 1987), 255. All subsequent references to the *Federalist Papers* in this chapter are from this edition.

14. John F. Kennedy, *Profiles in Courage* (New York: Harper & Brothers, 1956).

15. *Federalist* 71, 410.

16. *Federalist* 57, 343.

17. *Federalist* 68, 394.

18. Ibid., 394–395.

19. *Federalist* 73, 419.

20. *Federalist* 68, 393.

21. This process was amended with the Twelfth Amendment, though the general point about the deliberative nature of the system remained unchanged. See the first appendix to this volume.

22. *Federalist* 10, 123.

23. Ibid., 127.

24. *Federalist* 68, 393.

25. *Federalist* 47, 303.

Chapter II
The Development and Democratization of the Electoral College
Andrew E. Busch

1. Roughly speaking, because states with an equal number of electoral votes can still vary significantly in population.

2. Madison explicitly referred to the Electoral College as "a very compound source" of the president's powers, since "[t]he immediate election of the President is to be made by the states in their political characters. The votes allotted to them are in a compound ratio, which considers them partly as distinct and coequal societies, partly as unequal members of the same society." James Madison, *Federalist* 39, ed. Clinton Rossiter, *The Federalist Papers*

(New York: New American Library, 1961), 244. All subsequent references to the *Federalist Papers* in this chapter are from this edition.

3. James W. Ceaser, *Presidential Selection: Theory and Development* (Princeton, N.J.: Princeton University Press, 1979), 41–87.

4. Alexander Hamilton in *Federalist* 68 argued that it was "desirable that the immediate election be made by men most capable of analyzing the qualities adapted to the station and acting under circumstances favorable to deliberation, and to a judicious combination of all the reasons and inducements which were proper to govern their choice. A small number of persons, selected by their fellow-citizens from the general mass, will be most likely to possess the information and discernment requisite to so complicated an investigation" (see Appendix II). Yet Hamilton also made it clear that "the people themselves" were decisive.

5. James Bryce, *The American Commonwealth* (Chicago: Charles H. Sergel and Co., 1891), vol. 1, 38.

6. Paul F. Boller Jr., *Presidential Campaigns* (New York: Oxford University Press, 1984), 9.

7. For a brief moment in 1960, some Southern Democrats ran slates of unpledged electors in hopes of holding the balance between Nixon and Kennedy in the Electoral College. All eight of Mississippi's winning electors and six of Alabama's 11 were unpledged, ultimately voting for Senator Harry Byrd of Virginia. Nevertheless, the unpledged elector movement failed to achieve its objective, and the experiment was not repeated. It can also be argued that the Strom Thurmond "Dixiecrat" campaign of 1948 and the George Wallace campaign of 1968, while superficially seeking to elect Thurmond and Wallace, were actually "unpledged elector" movements in disguise. In both cases, the real objective seems to have been to win enough electoral votes to hold the balance between the two major parties and then throw support to whichever one appeared more pliant.

8. Bryce, *American Commonwealth*, vol. 1, 38.

9. This development was a twentieth-century phenomenon. In 1940, only 15 states used the "short ballot"; by 1980, 38 states did. Another 11 list both candidates and electors. Only one (Mississippi) automatically lists only electors, though electors can choose to publish a candidate identification. See Lawrence D. Longley and Neal R. Peirce, *The Electoral College Primer 2000* (New Haven, Conn.: Yale University Press, 1999), 107–108.

10. In a situation with some parallels, the Louisiana legislature in 1960 briefly

considered seating an unpledged slate of electors in place of the slate of Kennedy electors who were actually elected. Under severe criticism, it abandoned the idea.

11. Despite the general ticket system, it was still possible on rare occasions for a state to split its electoral votes. This occurred in states where voters had to vote for each elector separately. Because the votes for each of a party's electors might not be exactly the same, it was possible in very close elections for the generally losing party to place its top vote-getting elector above the winning party's lowest vote-getting elector. This phenomenon is, of course, impossible in states that have adopted the "short ballot." See *Congressional Quarterly's Guide to U.S. Elections* (Washington, D.C.: Congressional Quarterly, 1975), 6–7.

12. See Judith Best, *The Case Against Direct Election of the President* (Ithaca, N.Y.: Cornell University Press, 1975), 22–23; see also Neal R. Peirce and Lawrence D. Longley, *The People's President: The Electoral College in American History and the Direct Vote Alternative* (New Haven, Conn.: Yale University Press, 1981), 37, 46–47.

13. Jackson's lead in the popular vote, however, was not a true national aggregate because six of 24 states still selected their electors by state legislative action and hence reported no popular vote. Among those six was New York, by far the most populous state in the Union.

14. Stephen J. Wayne, *The Road to the White House 2000: The Politics of Presidential Elections* (New York: Bedford St. Martin's, 2001), 15.

15. The congressional caucus was a mode of presidential nomination used by the parties from 1800 through 1824. Each party's members of Congress would meet to designate their presidential nominees. When the Federalist Party collapsed after 1816, nomination by the caucus was tantamount to election. In the absence of two-party competition, however, party discipline declined and the caucus imploded. In 1824, fewer than half of the congressmen attended the Republican caucus, which then nominated the relatively unpopular William Crawford of Georgia. Other candidates with broader national support, including John Quincy Adams, Andrew Jackson, and Henry Clay, ran anyway and were nominated by state legislatures or conventions. The caucus's inability to prevent this profusion of candidates accounted for the four-way split in the Electoral College that sent the decision of 1824 to the House. The caucus also suffered from the defect of placing presidential selection in the hands of the legislative branch, violating the principle of separation of powers.

16. Boller, 136.

17. The December 12 "safe harbor" deadline played a major role in the U.S. Supreme Court's *Bush v. Gore* decision declaring that the Florida Supreme Court had run out of time to impose a new vote-counting regime. Prior to that decision, speculation centered on the possibility that the Florida legislature would name a slate of Bush electors at the same time Florida courts would declare Gore electors to have won. In that case, the dispute would be settled by Congress in accord with the post-*Hayes v. Tilden* legislation. If both houses did not agree on which slate to accept, the decision would have reverted to the state's executive. In addition, the challenge provisions of the law were actually utilized in 1969, when Sen. Edmund Muskie (D-Maine) and Rep. James G. O'Hara (D-Mich.), joined by six other Senators and 37 other Representatives, objected that the vote of North Carolina elector Lloyd W. Bailey was not "regularly given" because he had voted for George Wallace despite having been pledged to Richard Nixon. The motion failed and in any event would not have affected the election outcome.

18. In Alabama, five of the 11 winning electors were pledged to Kennedy, but the other six winners ran as unpledged Democratic electors and in fact did not vote for Kennedy. Thus, it can be argued that Kennedy should not be credited with the full vote total achieved by his top vote-getting elector in Alabama, but rather with only 5/11ths of that total. Were one to make this adjustment, it would place Kennedy's national popular vote total below Nixon's. See Peirce and Longley, *The People's President*, 65–67; Walter McDougall, "The Slippery Statistics of the Popular Vote," *New York Times*, 16 November 2000, A35.

19. Maine adopted this reform in 1969, Nebraska in 1992. However, neither has actually split its electoral votes in an election held under these rules.

20. See Richard E. Cohen and Louis Jacobson, "Can It Be Done?" *The National Journal*, 18 November 2000, 3659; *Who Should Elect the President?* (Washington, D.C.: League of Women Voters, 1969), 91–144. For a summary of reform efforts through history, see Peirce and Longley, *The People's President*, 131–180.

21. On 1968, see *Who Should Elect the President?* 98. A series of polls taken after election day 2000 showed a national popular vote supported by 57, 61, and 62 percent of Americans. See Tom Hamburger and Joni James, "Its Role in Question, Electoral College Picks Bush," *Wall Street Journal*, 19 December 2000, A22; "Poll Track: The Electoral College," *National Journal*, 18 November 2000, 3667.

22. An example could be seen after the 2000 election when one academic critic referred to the Electoral College as "the system established by our founding fathers, who feared the people and favored elites like themselves" (Michael Cummings, "Reforming Electoral Democracy," *Denver Post*, 28 January 2001, 6G).

23. Peirce and Longley, *The People's President*, 22.

Chapter III
Federalism, the States, and the Electoral College
JAMES R. STONER JR.

1. See, for example, Neal R. Pierce, *The People's President: The Electoral College in American History and the Direct-Vote Alternative* (New York: Simon and Schuster, 1968), 25-26; but cf. Alexander Bickel, *The New Age of Political Reform: The Electoral College, the Convention, and the Party System* (New York: Harper & Row, 1968), 17-18.

2. Sanford Levinson et al., "What We'll Remember in 2050: 9 Views on *Bush v. Gore*," *Chronicle of Higher Education*, 2 January 2001.

3. See, for example, essays that appeared immediately after the election by E.J. Dionne Jr. and Akil Reed Amar, reprinted in E.J. Dionne Jr. and William Kristol, eds., *Bush v. Gore: The Court Cases and the Commentary* (Washington, D.C.: Brookings Institution Press, 2001), 165-66, 171-72. According to the U.S. Census Bureau's analysis of apportionment of the House for the 108th Congress (which begins in 2003), states that went for Gore will lose seven seats and thus electoral votes, while the Bush states will net a gain of seven.

4. The former view is widely argued today, and seems an obvious inference from the fact that every state is apportioned three votes before the differences in their populations are considered; the latter view considers the effectiveness of each vote under the winner-take-all system, which makes winning at least several of the most populous states essential to any successful campaign. See J.F. Banzhaf III, "One Man, 3,312 Votes: A Mathematical Analysis of the Electoral College," *Villanova Law Review* 13 (1968): 308-346.

5. See, for example, Alexis Simending, James A. Barnes, and Carl M. Cannon, "Pondering a Popular Vote: A Detailed Look at What Might Be Gained, and Lost, if We Abolished the Electoral College," *National Journal*, 18 November 2000, 3650-56.

6. Pierce, *The People's President*, Appendix B, 309-11.

7. Sidney M. Milkis and Michael Nelson, *The American Presidency: Origins and*

Development, 1776–1990 (Washington, D.C.: Congressional Quarterly Press, 1990), 120.

8. See "Letters from the Federal Farmer," no. 8, and "Essays of Brutus," nos. 3–4, in Herbert Storing, ed., *The Anti-Federalist: Writings by the Opponents of the Constitution* (Chicago: University of Chicago Press, 1985), 73–79, 122–132.

Chapter IV
Moderating the Political Impulse
PAUL A. RAHE

1. For a detailed, accurate, and invaluable account of the operation of this system, see Walter Berns, "How the Electoral College Works," in *After the People Vote: A Guide to the Electoral College*, revised and enlarged edition, ed. Walter Berns (Washington, D.C.: The AEI Press, 1992), 3–31.

2. For a brief discussion of three of the four previous occasions when this may have taken place, see Norman J. Ornstein, "Three Disputed Elections," in *After the People Vote*, 35–43. It is worth noting that, in 1824, in a number of states, there was no popular vote, the electors being chosen by the legislatures; and that, in 1876, the scale and scope of voter intimidation and overall fraud rules out our being confident whether Rutherford B. Hayes or Samuel Tilden actually polled more votes. In 2000, we can no more be certain that Al Gore received a plurality of the votes cast in the country as a whole than that George W. Bush did so in Florida: in both venues, the margin of victory fell within the statistical margin of error. The only election in which we can be confident that the president selected lost the popular vote is that of 1888, when Benjamin Harrison defeated Grover Cleveland.

3. For an account of earlier attempts at reforming or eliminating the Electoral College, see Neal R. Peirce and Lawrence D. Longley, *The People's President: The Electoral College in American History and the Direct-Vote Alternative* (New York: Simon and Schuster, 1968), 58–204 (esp. 151–204).

4. See *Electing the President: A Report of the Commission on Electoral College Reform* (Chicago: American Bar Association, 1967), *passim* (esp. 3).

5. See U. S. House of Representatives, Ninety-First Congress, First Session, Committee on the Judiciary, *Electoral College Reform: Hearings on H. J. Res. 179, H. J. Res. 181, and Similar Proposals to Amend the Constitution Relating to Electoral College Reform, February 5, 6, 19, 20, 27; March 5, 6, 12, and 13, 1969* (Washington, D.C.: U.S. Government Printing Office, 1969) 172–209, 232–234, 433–438, 502–504, 507–520, 536–554, 653–657; and U. S. Senate, Ninety-First Congress, Second Session, Committee on the Judiciary, *Electoral*

Ninety-First Congress, Second Session, Committee on the Judiciary, *Electoral College Reform: Hearings on Amending the Constitution Relating to Electoral College Reform, April 15, 16, and 17, 1970* (Washington, D.C.: U. S. Government Printing Office, 1970) 191–247, 291–348. The League of Women Voters published a volume discussing the various proposals and their history: see *Who Should Elect the President?* (Washington, D.C.: League of Women Voters, 1969).

6. For the majority and minority reports, see U. S. Senate, Ninety-First Congress, Second Session, Committee on the Judiciary, *Direct Popular Election of the President: Report together with Individual, Separate, and Minority Views [To Accompany S. J. Res. 1]*, 14 August 1970, S. Rpt. 91-1123, Serial Set 12881-4 (Washington, D.C.: Government Printing Office, 1970).

7. Where the federal constitution allocated an equal number of seats in the U.S. Senate to each state, some state constitutions on the same logic allocated an equal number of seats in their state senates to each county. In a highly arbitrary decision based on a strained and implausible interpretation of the equal protection clause of the federal constitution's Fourteenth Amendment, the Supreme Court ruled in *Baker v. Carr* that representation in both state houses must be based on population.

8. Alexander M. Bickel, *The New Age of Political Reform: The Electoral College, the Convention, and the Party System* (New York: Harper & Row, 1968), 10.

9. This unwillingness to contemplate or incapacity to comprehend the possibility that there are occasions when, for the sake of good government, the democratic principle should in modest ways give ground to the dictates of political prudence is strikingly evident in the majority report issued in 1970 by the Senate Committee on the Judiciary: see *Direct Popular Election of the President*, 1–14, or go to www.claremont.org/publications/direct popularmaj.cfm.

10. For a thorough discussion, see Judith Best, *The Case Against Direct Election of the President: A Defense of the Electoral College* (Ithaca, N.Y.: Cornell University Press, 1975). See also Michael M. Uhlmann's essay in Chapter 7. The proposal advanced in 1969–70 was revived after the 1976 election by President Jimmy Carter and Senator Birch Bayh. Their effort impelled Martin Diamond to publish a point-by-point refutation of the charges laid against the Electoral College by the commission of the American Bar Association: see Diamond, *The Electoral College and the American Idea of Democracy* (Washington, D.C.: The AEI Press, 1977). Diamond's essay is reprinted in *After the People Vote*, 44–68.

11. *Congressional Record*, Vol. 102, Pt. 4, 84th Cong., 2d sess. (1956), 5150.

12. For the pertinent evidence with regard to their deliberations, see *The Records of the Federal Convention*, ed. Max Farrand (New Haven: Yale University Press, 1966), *passim* (esp. vol. 1, 52, 65–69, 80–81, 85, 88, 97, 175–76, 242, 292, 343, 447–48, 483; and vol. 2, 15, 29–35, 52–59, 64, 95, 101–103, 108–115, 120, 140, 151, 171, 175, 185, 201–208, 216, 401–404, 500–501, 511–515, 521–527, 535–537). The fact that a great many options were at various times under consideration is a sign neither of confusion nor of profound disagreement on the part of the Framers. From their perspective, the appropriate institutional arrangements regarding the presidency depended on the arrangements regarding the legislative and judicial branches of government. A decision with regard to one branch of government required rethinking the arrangements with regard to the others.

13. Thomas Jefferson made this point early with considerable force: see his *Notes on the State of Virginia*, ed. William Peden (New York: Norton, 1972), query 13. His argument was later taken up by James Madison: see *The Federalist*, ed. Jacob E. Cooke (Middletown, Conn.: Wesleyan University Press, 1961), no. 48.

14. To a more considerable degree than we can easily imagine, they succeeded: see Ralph Ketcham, *Presidents Above Party: The First American Presidency, 1789–1826* (Chapel Hill: University of North Carolina Press, 1984).

15. The best study, by far, both of the deliberations by which the Framers felt their way towards consensus on this question and of the intentions underlying the institutional logic they eventually inscribed within the selection process is Paul Eidelberg, *The Philosophy of the American Constitution* (New York: The Free Press, 1968), 166–201.

16. Under the provisions of the Constitution ratified in 1788–1789, the finalists were to be the five candidates who received the most votes in the Electoral College. This number was subsequently reduced to three by the Twelfth Amendment, which is reprinted in Appendix 1 of this volume.

17. See *Federalist* 68, which is reprinted in Appendix 2.

18. For a careful discussion of what actually happened in the various presidential elections in this regard and a detailed analysis of the circumstances militating against a candidate winning a majority within the Electoral College while losing in the popular vote, see Best, *The Cases Against Direct Election of the President*, 46–123.

19. The exception proves the rule: it took a civil war to establish the one-

party system in the South and to give the Republican Party sufficient leverage elsewhere to enable it to preserve its hegemony without ever having to rely on southern support.

20. For the pertinent Congressional testimony in 1969, see U. S. House of Representatives, *Electoral College Reform*, 286–297, 380–393. For the statement endorsed by the NAACP in 1977, see U.S. House of Representatives, Subcommittee on the Constitution of the Committee on the Judiciary, Ninety-Fifth Congress, First Session, *The Electoral College and Direct Election: Hearings on the Electoral College and Direct Election of the President and Vice President (S. J. Res. 1, 8, and 18), July 20, 22, 28, and August 2, 1977: Supplement* (Washington, D.C.: U. S. Government Printing Office, 1977), 255–256.

21. His testimony can be found in U.S. Senate, *Electoral College Reform*, 67–75.

22. See U.S. Senate, *The Electoral College and Direct Election: Supplement*, 256–257.

23. On this point, see the useful discussion in Best, *The Case Against Direct Election of the President*, 191–204.

24. Arthur Schlesinger Jr., "Fixing the Electoral College," *The Washington Post*, 19 December 2000, A39.

25. See Nelson W. Polsby, "The Electoral College," *Political Promises: Essays and Commentaries on American Politics* (New York: Oxford University Press, 1974), 160–164 (esp. 161).

26. Their views were appended to the majority report issued that year by the Senate Committee on the Judiciary: see *Direct Popular Election of the President*, 16.

27. See Andrew Burstein, *America's Jubilee: How in 1826 a Generation Remembered Fifty Years of Independence* (New York: Alfred A. Knopf, 2001), 159–204.

28. Jack Rakove, "The Accidental Electors," *The New York Times*, 19 December 2000, A35.

29. For a defense of the latter proposal on these very grounds, see Grover Norquist, "The Coming Bush Dynasty," *The American Spectator* 34, no. 1 (February 2001): 58–59.

30. See Ralph Rossum, "The Irony of Constitutional Democracy: Federalism, the Supreme Court, and the Seventeenth Amendment," *San Diego Law Review* 36, no. 3 (1999): 671–741.

31. See *Federalist* 39.

32. Schlesinger, "Fixing the Electoral College," A39.

33. See U.S. Senate, *Electoral College Reform*, 140–149.

Chapter VI

The Electoral College and the Uniqueness of America
DANIEL PATRICK MOYNIHAN

1. An earlier version of this essay was delivered on the floor of the United States Senate, June 27, 1979, to address Senate Joint Resolution 28, an attempt to abolish the Electoral College and replace it with a national popular election for president followed by a run-off election if no candidate received at least 40 percent of the votes.

Chapter VII

Creating Constitutional Majorities: The Electoral College after 2000
MICHAEL M. UHLMANN

1. This chapter is a revised version of the article "As the College Goes, So Goes the Constitution," first published in the Winter 2001 edition of the *Claremont Review of Books*. © 2001 The Claremont Institute for the Study of Statesmanship and Political Philosophy. Reprinted by permission. All rights reserved.

Appendix I

1. The material in brackets has been superseded by the Twelfth Amendment.

2. The part in brackets has been superseded by section 3 of the Twentieth Amendment.

About the Contributors

MICHAEL BARONE is Senior Writer at *U.S. News & World Report* and principal co-author of *The Almanac of American Politics*, which has been published in new editions every two years for three decades. He is also the author of *Our Country: The Shaping of America from Roosevelt to Reagan* and has provided political commentary on numerous television programs.

WALTER BERNS is Resident Scholar at the American Enterprise Institute and John M. Olin Professor Emeritus at Georgetown University. He is the author or editor of seven books, including *After the People Vote: Steps in Choosing the President*, *Taking the Constitution Seriously*, and *The First Amendment and the Future of American Democracy*.

ANDREW E. BUSCH is an Associate Professor of Political Science at the University of Denver. He has authored or co-authored six books on American politics and elections, including *Horses in Midstream: U.S.*

Midterm Elections and Their Consequences, 1894-1998 and *The Perfect Tie: The True Story of the 2000 Presidential Election* (with James W. Ceaser).

GARY L. GREGG II holds the Mitch McConnell Chair in Leadership at the University of Louisville, where he is also director of the McConnell Center for Political Leadership. An award-winning teacher and former National Director of the Intercollegiate Studies Institute, he is author or editor of five books, including *Vital Remnants: America's Founding and the Western Tradition* and *Patriot Sage: George Washington and the American Political Tradition* (with Matthew Spalding).

MITCH MCCONNELL has served in the United States Senate since 1984, when he became the first Kentucky Republican to win a statewide race in thirty years. He is chairman of the powerful Senate Rules Committee, which gave him the responsibility of orchestrating the transfer of power during the 2001 presidential inauguration. Kentucky's Senior Senator, he has been named by publications such as *George* magazine and *Congressional Quarterly* as one of the most powerful people in Washington.

DANIEL PATRICK MOYNIHAN was a member of the United States Senate from 1977-2001. With a public service career extending over four decades, he served in the Kennedy, Johnson, and Nixon Administrations before becoming Ambassador to India and then Ambassador to the United Nations in the 1970s. He was first elected to the United States Senate as a Democrat from New York in 1976. A former professor at Harvard University, his many books include *Family and Nation, Came the Revolution,* and *On the Law of Nations.*

PAUL A. RAHE is Jay P. Walker Professor of American History at the University of Tulsa. His book *Republics Ancient and Modern: Classical Republicanism and the American Revolution*, which appeared in 1992, has now been made available in a three-volume paperback edition from the University of North Carolina Press.

JAMES R. STONER JR. is Associate Professor of Political Science at Louisiana State University and is author of *Common Law and Liberal Theory: Coke, Hobbes, and the Origins of American Constitutionalism*. He is currently completing major studies of the influence of common law on American constitutionalism and on the theoretical underpinnings of assertions of judicial supremacy in America.

MICHAEL M. UHLMANN is Senior Vice-President of the Lynde and Harry Bradley Foundation. For many years an adjunct professor of government at Claremont McKenna College, he authored the Minority Report of the Senate Judiciary Committee in 1970 in opposition to direct election of the president. He later served as Assistant Attorney General for Legislative Affairs (1975–1977) and as Special Assistant to President Ronald Reagan (1981–1984).

Index